THE BRITISH PEOPLE AT WAR

Contents

ODHAMS PRESS LTD., LONG ACRE, LONDON, W.C.2

To all who
work and suffer
in the cause
of Freedom—
this book is
dedicated

THE RT. HON. WINSTON S. CHURCHILL, C.H., M.P.

From a portrait specially painted for this work by
A. R. THOMSON, A.R.A.

The British People go to War

AT 11.0 a.m. on September 3rd, 1939, Britain entered a new era. The transition from peace to war was swift and dramatic. The country had put on uniform. The sky, over the cities was dotted with balloons. Everywhere, people were digging trenches, filling sandbags. Gas masks were being given out. There was a rush for black paper and cloth to screen windows and skylights. Grim, grey vehicles thundered along the roads on mysterious errands. There was in the air a feeling of change, complete, inevitable, tremendous.

Every British household had felt war was brewing though none could anticipate exactly what it would be like. Now, in their quiet way, the people got busy. There was work to do, no time to waste in regrets for week-ends by the sea, quiet evenings at home, tennis, bridge-parties, and all the rest of the pleasant little details of their previous existence. The world might be upside down. If so, they must learn to be upside down too. They must do all sorts of things they had never done before. They must adapt themselves to conditions that had never existed before at all. They did all this with cheerfulness for they saw that it was necessary. The British might be a little weak on geography and the nicer distinctions of

3

SWIFT IN ATTACK
The fighter planes come and go on
their task of sweeping the skies.

political theories: but they were quite clear on the difference between being free men and women and being slaves. The totalitarian powers of Europe had put the issue before them and as the free people of a democratic state they had made the choice deliberately.

The subsequent adventures of the average and representative citizen may be followed in these pages. The boys are in the Army, Navy or Air Force. The girls are on the land, in the munition factories, in one of the uniformed, auxiliary services. The elders are Air Raid Wardens or Home Guards. They are defenders of the Home Front—a phrase which has a literal meaning for the island of Britain itself is in the front line. Its cities are liable to daily attack, its coasts are rimmed with danger.

To look through these photographs is to recapture successive thrills of the war—the queer unreality of the sunny morning in September when the ultimatum to Germany expired, the early discomforts of the blackout, the shock and the prompt rally after it that followed the news of Dunkirk, the speed with which a great volunteer army came into being, the brief, intense drama of air battles over Britain, the fantastic scenes in the Tube where tired Londoners sought for sleep, the gallant epic of fire-fighting and rescue in the Blitz.

In addition there is here a panorama of the daily life and doings of the people. They have made Britain into a giant airfield; a vast training ground where the technique of war is learnt; they pile up the munitions in the factories; turn over the land that had never previously known the plough; lay down the keels of new ships in an unpausing succession.

In days to come many things appearing in these pictures will be of historic interest. It may be that the last word in mechanical progress (as it appeared at the time) in those future days will look rather primitive. As the plane of 1914 was to the giant bomber of the Second World War, so will this be in turn to the 250-seat, round-the-world airliner of to-morrow. The dwellers in replanned cities will look with curious interest at the ruins and smouldering debris, on which, phœnix-like, new buildings have arisen. At the same time this family album (so indeed it may be called), for never was the nation more closely united, has one thing in it without date—that is the spirit of the British people, who acted, under unprecedented circumstances, just as might be expected from their tradition.

STEADY IN DEFENCE
The crews stand to the anti-aircraft guns on the Home Front.

CRISIS

POLAND INVADED
Several Towns Bombed

AS THE WAR CLOUDS GATHERED FAST . . .

The summer of 1939 was electric with foreboding. The Continent of Europe was an armed camp. Hitler's attitude towards Poland gave no hint of peaceful settlement though it was not until September 1st that hope was abandoned of keeping peace. Meanwhile Britain's forces were quietly mustered. Thousands of Naval reservists had reported at the naval depots of Portsmouth, Devonport and Chatham, bringing Britain's Reserve Fleet up to war strength. The Army, likewise was mobilized, and fixed bayonets, steel helmets and gas masks were now familiar sights. These photographs of the summer of 1939 form a background to the intense unrest in Europe fomented by the Nazi plotters of war and charged with menace.

WAR IS
DECLARED

WHEN BRITAIN'S ULTIMATUM EXPIRED. 11 a.m., SEPT. 3, 1939

That the British Government regarded war as almost inevitable might be gathered from the passing of the Emergency Powers Act on August 24 : and after Hitler invaded Poland the public felt the issue decided. The crowd stood tense and still in Parliament Square as Big Ben struck eleven on the fateful and brilliantly fine morning of September 3rd—the hour at which Britain's ultimatum to Germany expired. The tension and the change of mood as the deep chime ceased to vibrate are written in the photographs then taken. Here, at last, was decision. On the faces of the people streaming away from Downing Street there is relief—a calm and serious determination to see the thing through. They disperse quietly, each already thinking of some war job to be done. The King broadcast on this day : "There may be dark days ahead and war can no longer be confined to the battlefield. But we can only do the right as we see the right." To all, the cause was clear.

WHEN THE FIRST SIREN SOUNDED

A few minutes after eleven o'clock had struck, the whooping, wailing sound of the air-raid siren—heard already in practice tests but now invested with a sinister reality—warned London of the menace to be expected from the air. Without fuss, even with smiles, and with curiosity as to what would happen next rather than fear, the people made for the shelters which were already in being. There was confidence that our defences were in good order. The little group shown below was snapped in Whitehall on the morning of September 3rd. The first siren was a false alarm—some time was yet to elapse before the real test came to Britain.

LOOKING AFTER THE CHILDREN

To get the children out of harm's way was, of course, one of the early duties of war-time. Children remaining in the towns were carefully shepherded into shelters like those seen above, though evacuation to safe areas was strongly urged on parents and measures were taken for a wholesale redistribution of young folk.

PRE-WAR PICCADILLY—A last look at the familiar blaze of light in the Circus.

PICCADILLY IN THE BLACKOUT—Eros aims his arrows in darkness more complete than he has ever known.

JOURNEY HOME—Windows were screened and a dim funnel of light fell on the passenger's newspaper.

PATTERNS OF WARTIME—White lines for traffic, windows boarded and papered against bomb blast.

EVACUATION IN PROGRESS

Plans to forestall a possible dislocation in town life by wholesale evacuation were ready before the outbreak of war, and were put into effect as soon as Germany invaded Poland. The migration of children was organized and carried through within four days and without a single accident. Mothers and children were billeted in private houses, the average cost to the Government of billeting schoolchildren being roughly nine shillings per child. This is said to have required more organization than the number of troops transported at that time to France. Scenes like those illustrated here, suggesting a holiday excursion on a large scale (except for the anxiety of parting) were frequent, though the scheme was not supported to anything like the extent provided for. February, 1940, saw a Second Evacuation Plan launched; June, 1940, a scheme for overseas evacuation; but there was no mass movement from the cities until the blitz period of September, 1940, when the population of London fell by a third. The children who stayed in the country, however, settled down happily, and gained notably in weight, size and general health, benefiting, also, from their introduction to rural work.

Evacuee twins ready to make a start, and a little Lambeth family settling down happily in Devonshire.

Complete with gas masks and labels the town children entrain for their extended holiday.

GUNS THAT DEFEND THE SHORES AND SHIPS OF BRITAIN

Guarding Britain's Life-lines

IN peace-time it was taken for granted that the ships of Britain sailed with merchandise to the ends of the earth, and returned home laden with an immense variety of luxuries and necessities for use and enjoyment. The highways of the sea are arteries through which the very lifeblood of Britain flows. It was not realized how open they were to attack until the prowling submarines fell like jackals on many defenceless ships, and the nation began to feel the stranglehold tightening about its throat. Then Britain woke up.

Many of the lessons of the last war had been forgotten. One, at least, was remembered. Ships travelling alone were easy prey for marauding enemy submarines and surface vessels. Convoys could be protected.

Theoretically, the convoy system is simplicity itself. A number of ships travelling to the same destination sail together under naval escort. Every ship keeps the same speed at a measured distance from its neighbour. All in the convoy follow a zig-zag route dictated by the commander of the escorting naval force—which scours the sea for submarines and surface raiders.

It sounds easy—but what a vast organization is needed to make it work ! The amount of essential traffic that must at all costs be kept moving is enormous. Its variety is bewildering. Troops, guns, ammunition and sup- plies of tens of thousands of items of military equipment must flow in a steady stream to every theatre of war overseas. Petrol, oil, food, raw materials of every kind and manufactured munitions of war from other countries must reach British ports. Count the number of ports about the coasts big enough to accommodate sea-going ships. Make a guess at the number of ships that must dock, discharge cargo, turn round and load again, every week. Think of their varying speeds, the many routes they have to take and the different distances of their several destinations. Then imagine how immensely intricate the system must be to ensure clockwork timing for every coming and going. It involves the Army, the Navy, the railway and dockyard systems of this country; shippers at home and overseas, and an unbelievably complicated network of cable and wireless communications between ships and ports throughout the world.

The war had not been many days old before the beginnings of the convoy organization were in working order. It grew fast. Soon the huge mass of traffic outstripped the Navy's resources of escort vessels, and merchantmen had to be armed so that they could protect themselves on journeys where no escort could be given them. Then to the menace of the submarine was added a new peril from the air—the enemy dive-bomber; and ships had to be equipped with captive balloons and anti-aircraft guns, whilst their crews were given intensive courses of training in the handling of their weapons.

The struggle became intenser and fiercer as the months passed; for it was literally a struggle for the life of a nation. The sea-lines were Britain's life-lines. They fed her citizens; they fed and armed her fighting men in other lands. Unless she kept them open she could not survive.

The dramatic pictures on the following pages give you glimpses of the struggle—and of the men who have borne the burden of it with uncomplaining endurance, and with quiet sustained courage.

Mine-sweeping trawler goes out to sea.

WORK OF THE LITTLE SHIPS

Hundreds of small craft are essential to attend on a battle fleet. Minesweepers form a fleet in themselves. The trawlers and drifters of the fishing industry, as in the war, 1914-18, were specially suitable for this service. In addition to these were former cross-channel boats and former paddle steamers—as well as navy craft whose design retained something of the lines of a fishing boat. A minesweeper's crew is here seen getting ready.

AT THE WHEEL ON BOARD A BRITISH BATTLESHIP

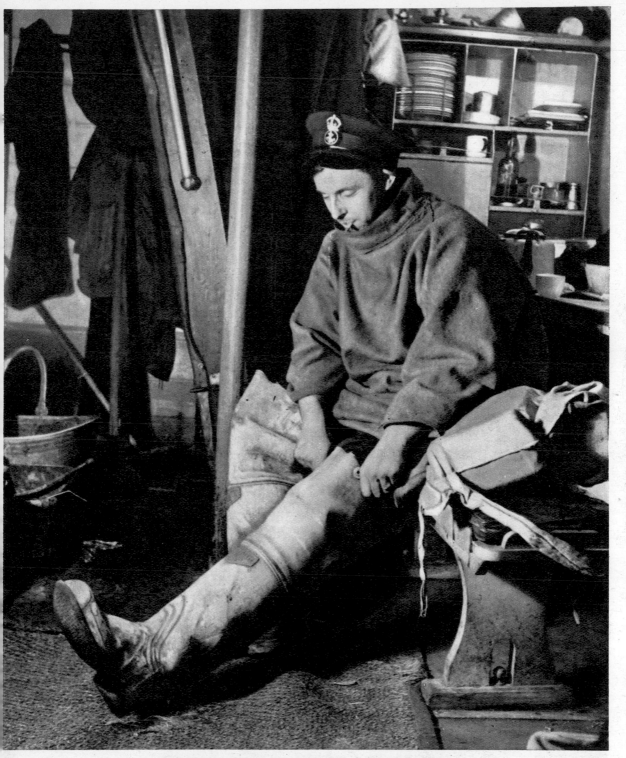

MEN WHO FIGHT THE BATTLE OF THE SEAS

With the outbreak of war every British sailor, whether in The Royal Navy or merchant service, became an active participant in the battle of the seas. Boats of every type from liners to trawlers were auxiliaries of the Navy itself, and throughout there was the same spirit of undemonstrative efficiency—from the bridge of the battleship to the little minesweeper. The quartermaster at the wheel knows his job. So also does the ex-fisherman, now one of thousands in the Royal Naval Patrol, who is pulling on his sea boots. In a few minutes' time he will be on the deck on watch against the dangers of mines and the attacks of a stealthy enemy.

THE NAVY'S WATCH ON SHIPPING

As the war progressed, attention became focused on the attacks made by U-boats on vessels of the United Nations. That enemy shipping had been largely swept from the seas was no longer prominent in people's minds because it was an accomplished fact. The power of the Royal Navy had been exerted none the less effectively because silently. Our photograph suggests the close scrutiny directed on all ships. During the first three months of war about 700,000 tons of suspected contraband were intercepted and 500,000 tons seized, including large quantities of petroleum, copper and cotton. The Navicert system, commercial passports issued by British representatives abroad, for cargoes which they approved before shipment, assisted in the efficacy of the blockade. "As in 1914-18," the German economic expert Emil Helferrich confessed, "England's power has brought the German overseas trade to a complete standstill. The tragedy of 1914-18 is being repeated." In other words the sea blockade by Britain was a fact of great importance, and the tonnage of Axis ships confiscated or sunk mounted up to a formidable total of millions. Some enemy ships might contrive to run the gauntlet and steal from port to port, but they were few in number.

MERCHANTMEN DOUBLY ARMED   Merchant ships must be defensively armed and that against enemies above and below. Therefore most ships were provided with two guns. That seen in the background is a 4-inch for use against submarines. In the foreground an anti-aircraft gun goes aboard.

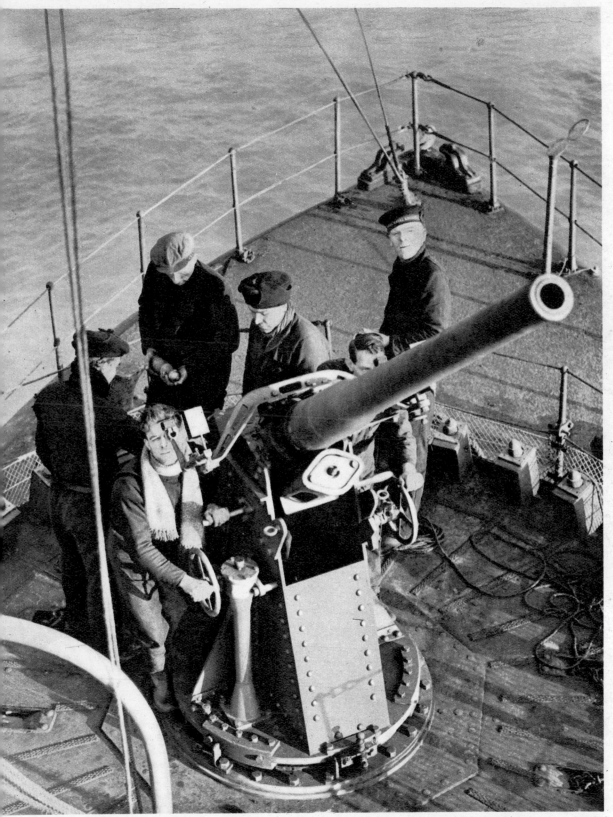

The twelve-pounder gun of a mine-sweeping trawler is brought into action when enemy aircraft are sighted off the East Coast. The British seamen under the instruction of specialists soon become able to handle the weapons provided and to "hit back".

ENEMY AIRCRAFT IN SIGHT

THE CAPTAINS ASSEMBLE

The illustrations on this page show above, the encounter of three captains of merchant ships who are sailing in convoy, types of the sturdy breed for whom neither the sea nor the enemy hold any terrors; and, below, the Captains' Conference, where a Naval officer explains to an attentive group the plan which the convoy will follow

BEFORE THE CONVOY SAILS

Towards the end of the last war convoys reached a highly effective level. In the renewed and still more relentless struggle they were organized with the greatest care and close collaboration between Navy, Air Force and Merchant Service. Greeting each other with a friendly grin, husky seasoned skippers would meet and listen at the Captains' Conference to the Naval officer's explanation of the convoy's time of sailing and formation. They would sit on benches in the Naval Control Office, as if in a schoolroom, taking in the crisp and exact instructions designed to guard against the threefold attacks of a wily enemy. When the conference was over the masters of the ships took their orders and studied them carefully, asking a question here and there. In the photograph above the ships are seen assembled with steam up, and a cover of balloons, ready to start at dawn. In all probability they will go through some exciting moments before they reach port again.

A picture of this kind gives a good idea of the vigilance required in watching over a convoy. The Navy woul[...] act very like a sheepdog rounding up the stragglers and keeping in constant touch with the flock. Straggling

was sometimes inevitable owing to differences of speed between ships, though as far as possible ships of the same size and speed were grouped together. Aircraft played their effective part as the eyes of the convoy.

31

WARTIME HAZARDS OF THE SEA

Never in its whole history was the story of the sea so full of hairsbreadth escape, of peril in every shape bravely encountered. In the Channel, ships had to meet bombing attacks and shelling from the French coast as well as the attacks of U-boats. In the Atlantic, distance from land or friendly ships added its own hazard. Rescue took many forms : Ships on patrol might come across the survivors of a torpedoed steamer, floating in an open boat. Lame ducks of a convoy would if possible be towed into port. Airmen too, might come down in the sea. Drifter, trawler, patrol boat, lifeboat, minesweeper, motor launch, destroyer and search aircraft formed a rescue system for them and, of course, for all in distress; while on shore the coastguards, the Royal Observer Corps (and general public too) kept a sharp lookout for any signs of the deadly drama enacted on the waters.

Shells bursting round convoyed vessels and their escort as they pass through the Channel.

A crippled member of a convoy is towed into harbour where the Admiralty Salvage Officer will take over.

CONVOY OFF THE COAST   The long line of vessels in convoy of varying shapes and sizes was a sight which might have been sung by Kipling. Here a convoy which has safely negotiated all the dangers of the route, is seen from the deck of an accompanying destroyer, approaching port.

A hundred million pounds' worth of supplies might come to Britain in a single convoy—guns, ammunition, raw materials, food stuffs—butter, bacon, lard, meat. Such a large convoy would be split up and unloaded in several ports to ensure a rapid turn round.

DELIVERING THE GOODS

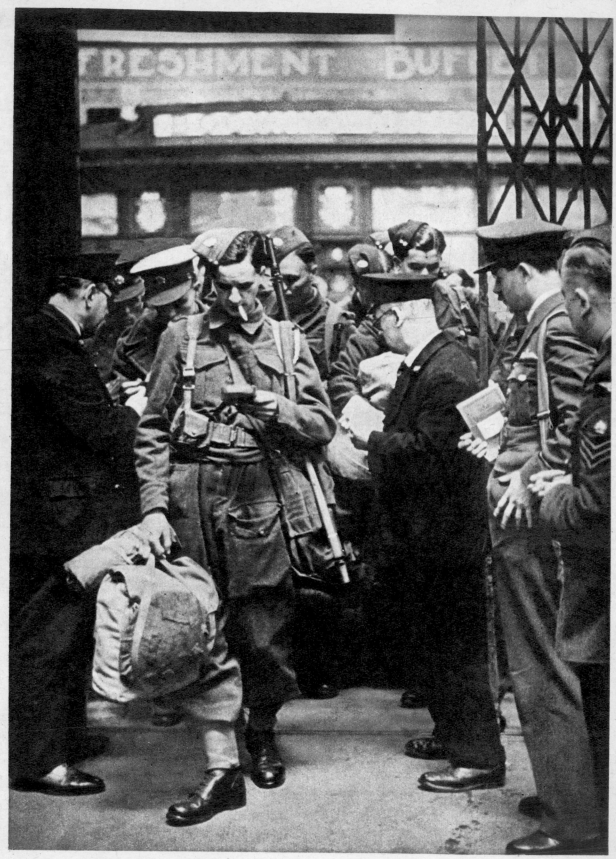

COMPLETELY EQUIPPED—AND ON THE THRESHOLD OF ADVENTURE

Making a Citizen Army

"TURNING the nation into an armed camp" is a phrase that is easy enough to say. But how many people realize that an army is, in simple fact, a self-contained, self-supporting organization as complete and complex as the nation for which it fights?

A fighting force sent into the field must be completely self-reliant. It feeds, clothes and doctors itself. It creates its own telephone, telegraph, wireless and postal systems. It makes its own roads and builds its own bridges. It lays its own railways and runs its own trains. Wherever it goes it takes its own supply organization to stock and distribute wherever they are required the one hundred thousand different items of equipment it needs—gun parts, wireless parts, vehicle spares, electrical and mechanical appliances, precision instruments, and every conceivable kind of merchandise from a pin to a steam roller.

Because it must depend on itself for everything it needs, before battle, in battle and after battle, an army must include in its personnel men trained in every art and science and skilled occupation, as well as in the grim business of making war; and before it can take these men from their civilian occupations, it must be ready to sort them out according to their abilities, find housing accommodation for them, and have ready the means by which they can be given the specialized training of fit and competent soldiers.

From the very beginning of the war, Britain determined that its resources of man-power must be diverted from the pursuits of peace to national service with all possible speed. It knew that its need was too urgent and imperative for the matter to be left to individual choice.

With the passing of the Compulsory Service Acts, the process of selection began. Age group by age group, men of all classes were required to register for the service of the nation. Those engaged in occupations essential for the maintenance of the community's life were "reserved." The rest were called to the colours as fast as the military organization could absorb, train and distribute them amongst its many corps and regiments.

Within a few months of the declaration of war, Britain became a vast training ground and a nerve-centre for the world-wide movement of armies.

The mechanization of military forces and the employment of methods of warfare hitherto unknown, brought training problems of their own. In addition to those required for all the ordinary duties of an army, men had to be found and trained for duties of new and exceptionally arduous kinds. Men specially selected for their powers of endurance and initiative were formed into regiments of "Commandos"—shock troops, capable of undertaking swift surprise raids on enemy territory. Others were trained to descend on enemy strongholds by parachute. Yet others were put through intensive courses of preparation to meet the first onslaughts of an invading force. Besides all these, selected groups of men were taken to remote places and instructed in work of a more delicate and secret kind, such as the manipulation of the amazing radio-location instruments which before long were called upon to play a decisive part in the aerial battles over Britain.

It was a mighty task, reviewed in the light of the nation's known unpreparedness at the time when it had to begin, yet it was done.

LANDING EXERCISE—The army perfects itself in the technique of modern war.

CALL FOR MAN POWER

More than 200,000 men between 20 and 21 registered in June, 1939, under the Military Training Act. Liability to serve in the armed forces was extended in September to all men between 18 and 41. The already greatly increased Territorial Army and Militia and the compulsory scheme together ensured that by October a million men were under intensive training in Great Britain. The complete outfit of an infantry man (redesigned since the war of 1914-18) cost approximately £20, included eighty items. Young men registering at the Labour Exchange, as seen above, could express preference for one of the services. Only a fraction of 1 per cent. were conscientious objectors. Army recruits went through the established routine of " parades " and drill movements, were made fit by scientific methods.

HOW THE SOLDIER GROWS FIT

The recruit plays and works hard. Formal exercises were replaced in the Second World War by games (like the basketball game pictured above) and P.T. had an element of play. Day by day also the men got hardened to the routine of a soldier's training, trench digging, bayonet practice, and drill movements hammered in until they became instinctive. This was the groundwork preparatory for the training in the specialized functions and new methods of modern war which demanded an entirely new standard of intelligence and initiative.

ROUTINE OF MILITARY TRAINING
Trench digging and bayonet practice.

The Royal Armoured Corps—a general term comprising the units handling mechanical vehicles—the Royal
Tank Regiment—descendant of the young Tank Corps of 1914-1918, and the former regiments of the horsed

THE MECHANIZED ARMY

cavalry (which still retained their traditional titles, badges of rank and battle honours) absorbed great numbers of men. They manned large, fast-moving, fighting vehicles, like the Valentine tanks, here seen in action.

43

A STRONG PULL ON A HEAVY GUN

When the threat of invasion revived as a live issue, defensive preparations were made accordingly, and both coastal and inland regions were provided with strong batteries at defensive points. Guns and yet more guns were wanted. Coast artillery had two rôles—to deal wholesale with invading forces and also to protect ports from the attacks of surface craft. Inland, heavy guns served as a defence against infantry and, especially, the tanks which had shown such surprising success on the Continent. Their position, by skilful camouflage, could be most effectively concealed. The number and kind of guns mounted at different places was of course governed by the importance of the place and the local probabilities of attack, a variety being in use from 15 in. down to the coastal 12-pounder. The photograph shows artillery sliding a new barrel into a heavy gun on an invasion site in Southern England. It gives some idea of the weight and size of the weapons which surrounded Britain with a ring of steel and also of the number of trained men required to handle them. Though, in the Battle of Britain, the projected invasion was limited to the air and defence became the task of the R.A.F., defence by land was ready, if the need arose, to play a powerful part.

MANŒUVRES—SOMEWHERE IN ENGLAND

Never before the Second World War had the practice of warfare been so swift or so much complicated by surprise tactics and weapons. Manœuvres in consequence became increasingly realistic to accustom the troops to unexpected conditions. The threat of invasion created special reasons for familiarizing the troops with battle in Britain. Large-scale operations were made as nearly as possible like the real thing, thousands of tanks and armoured cars taking part for days and nights on end without pause. Above, a reconnaissance party of the advancing forces, with an armoured car, have come through a smoke screen and encountered a wire road block.

"BATTLE" IN BRITAIN—The armoured cars and tanks of the "invader" dash past camouflaged supply lorries.

Troops (who seem to feel the situation well enough in hand to abandon cover) chase the retreating "foe."

WORLD-WIDE MOVEMENT OF TROOPS

From 1939 onwards Britain was not merely point of departure for France and Flanders, but landing stage in a world-wide movement extending from the frozen north to tropical deserts and swamps. The adventures of the British soldier began in familiar style with the arrival of an Expeditionary Force in France, 158,000 men being transported across the Channel within five weeks. But the following period of move and counter-move distributed troops more and more widely. After the seizure of Denmark they went to the Faroe Islands and Reykjavik, capital of Iceland. In April, 1940, they were fighting at Namsos and Narvik in Norway. The coming and going of Empire troops interlaced, Canadians arriving in Britain in December, 1939, Australians in Egypt and Palestine in February, 1940, while American troops arrived in England and Northern Ireland in 1942. A huge and undaunted army was back again on British soil, after the heroic episode of Dunkirk and the fall of France. A double problem remained—of guarding Britain against invasion and of entering the new theatres of war as they opened. Britain remained the nerve-centre of a new, immense system of military communication which was adapted to meet the need arising in any quarter of the globe at any time.

THEY HAD TO BE TOUGH

To train the soldier as an individual, to make him sufficiently tough in body to stand up to the severest physical conditions, to sharpen him in mind for making instant decision—such was the training of the Commandos—picked troops whose job was to strike and be gone. "Commando," name applied to the burgher raiding parties of the Boers, aptly fitted the tough, self-reliant men who must learn to climb cliffs through a smoke screen or drop down a steep slope into water and swim with helmet, rifles, ammunition and equipment, in fact face the worst surprises of geography or enemy action. The human element in war had taken on a new significance.

COMMANDOS IN TRAINING—A SWIM IN FULL KIT

51

TRAINING PARATROOPS

Early in 1941 it was revealed that Britain had her parachute troops—or Special Air Service Troops as they were officially termed. Nerve, skill, determination, intelligence, initiative was the combination required—and selection was stringent. Their special boots and helmets were designed for protection—their overalls to prevent any part of their equipment being entangled. Like aerial mushrooms, the parachutes float lightly down and (as it seems from a distance) slowly. From their folds on the ground spring up quick moving, determined men knowing their objective, making a dash for it without a moment's delay. Speed is the crux of the matter.

ARMY FROM THE CLOUDS—PRACTISING A MASS PARACHUTE DESCENT

After the evacuation—a transport leaving Dunkirk.

Back in Britain. Troops on the way home after Dunkirk.

ONCE MORE READY
Men of the Royal Marines in an invasion practice.

BRITAIN'S FIGHTING FORCES GAIN STRENGTH FROM EXPERIENCE

The two photographs opposite recall that historic episode, the evacuation of the British Expeditionary Force from Dunkirk between May 29th and June 3rd, 1940. The troops on board a transport take a last look back at the blazing French coast. The inimitable sang-froid of the British Tommy can be seen in the attitude of these men straight out of the inferno. Neither a defeat nor a victory but an extraordinarily cool process of extrication from an impossible position in the face of overwhelming odds, Dunkirk became an incentive to future action. One thing at least it had demonstrated; the ability of the forces to function by land, air and sea, in perfect co-operation. Every soldier was now more enthusiastic than before. On the foundations of this episode was laid the patient reconstruction and development of the British Army into a mighty force ready to open a "Second Front," and to invade at the right moment where invasion would be of decisive effect against the enemy.

BOMBING-UP A STIRLING—HEAVYWEIGHT OF THE AIR

The Mastery of the Air

BEFORE the Battle of Britain had run its course, it had become clear that the mastery of the air was being won by British airmen. At the outset relative strength in the air was an unknown quantity. No one quite knew in the early days of war how and when the test would come, or between what opposing forces. The result of the definite challenge was a triumphant vindication of the men, the methods and the machines of the Royal Air Force. Beginning as a small though highly efficient service, the Air Force was so organised as to be capable of enormous expansion on the most effective lines. Through the Air Council it was in direct contact with the Cabinet. The links of responsibility between Air Staff, Air Ministry and Service Organization were devised with the same care for co-ordination and smooth working as in some great industrial concern. The eight commands, operational and non-operational, had their definite jobs to do. Flying personnel were trained by the most exacting standards, and by a brilliant stroke of administration, training was shared with the U.S.A. and the Empire. In addition, the exercise of some hundred different trades for men and fifty for women was provided for, all these trades being necessary to maintenance.

Few would have believed in 1939, that within three years every day would bring to Britain reinforcements of mighty bombing planes, flown across the Atlantic in a few hours; that fighter planes would be numbered in tens of thousands, An unceasing process of evolution went on in the machines used, designs ever more closely fitted to their purpose replacing constantly the older types. The skill and spirit of the men remained at a steadily high level, though their numbers vastly increased. From the airfields of Britain they went across the narrow seas to sweep the skies over Europe — to turn against the enemy the offensive weapon on which he had counted and to destroy the central arsenals of terrorism.

SEEN FROM THE PILOT'S COCKPIT—LANCASTERS ON A DAYLIGHT RAID

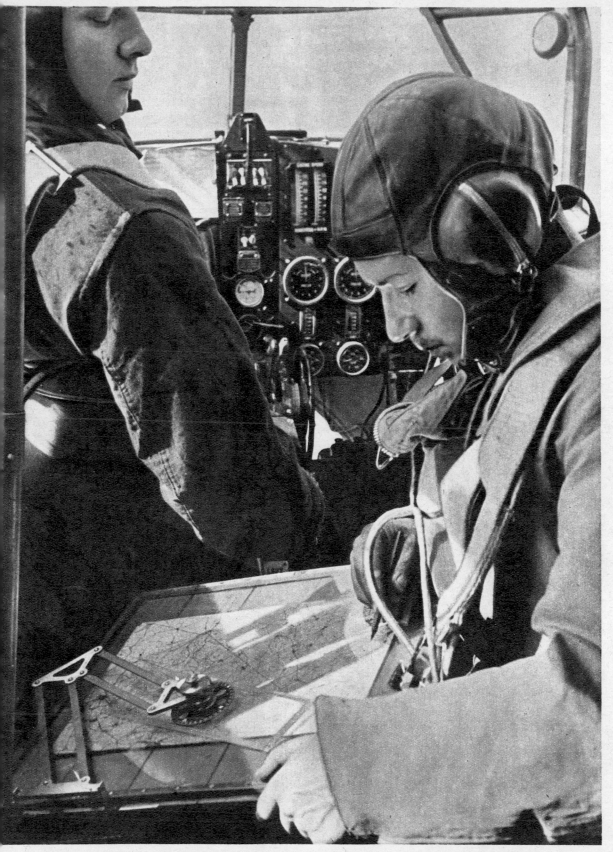

AIRMAN IN TRAINING—PILOT INSTRUCTOR AND PUPIL ON A NAVIGATION FLIGHT

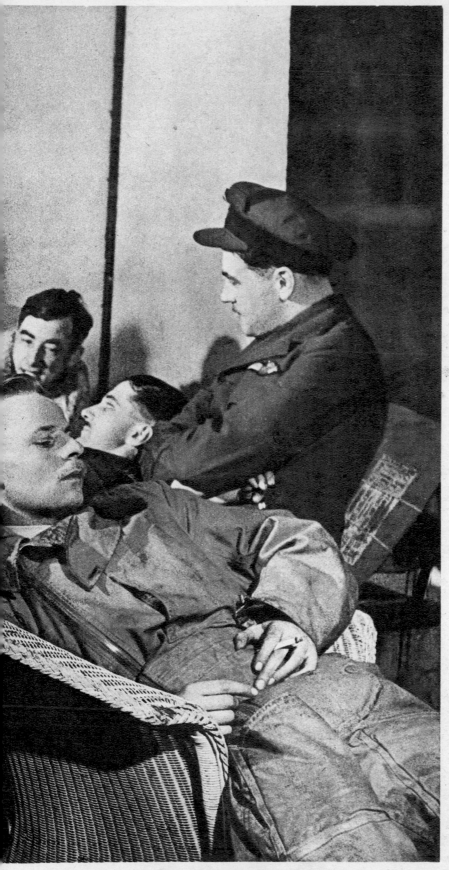

MEN LIKE THESE

Here is a typical scene in a dispersal hut showing members of a Fighter Squadron waiting for the call to action. Young men like these formed the barrier against which the full force of the Luftwaffe was hurled vainly. Their counterparts, the young German airmen, had anticipated a victory over "decadent" Britain, as easy as victory had been on the Continent. They fought with courage and tenacity but even so, and in spite of their superior numbers, they were crushingly defeated. The reason, basically, was the human element. Quality and number of machines counted, but quality of men turned the scale. The British airmen were able to hold on just the all important fraction longer, to act the all important fraction quicker. It is well to note that the flying men of the Royal Air Force represented no one class or status in civilian life. They were recruited from all grades and occupations. Outstanding physical fitness and intelligence were the factors that governed this selection. Efficiency was the code which they recognized, and no other. The general high standard of Britain's young men is reflected in the fact that the R.A.F.'s numbers could be enormously increased with no observable falling off in stamina or achievement on the part of this magnificent force.

(Photo: 'Life' Magazine)

Fighter pilots play shove ha'penny while they wait.

ELEMENTS O[

A machine 30 ft. long by 12 ft. high
with a wing span of some 40 ft.,
speed of between 3- and 400 mile[
per hour, a range of about 700 miles
an armament of machine gun[
firing 300 yards at 1200 rounds [
minute and cannon firing 60[
pounds weight up to 1000 yard[
Here is a rough average of the point[
(varying in detail with each) of [
fighter plane, Defiant, Beau[
fighter, Hurricane or Spitfire. [
young man, chosen for a tempera[
ment—quick and cool and traine[
to a hair—such is the fighter pilo[
In the dispersal hut of a fighte[
station (as seen at left), they awai[

FIGHTER COMMAND

the order from control to "scramble base." They play shove ha'penny and darts, drink lime juice (nothing stronger), while they wait: but are ready in a flash to be in their plane, day or night, with their 60 lbs. weight of equipment—helmet, parachute, "Mae West" life belt and folding dinghy. Above the clouds they fly in beautifully precise formation—in V shape, line abreast, or line astern (tactical unit in battle being two aircraft)—mark V Spitfires with cannon protruding from their wings being seen, line abreast, over a floor of clouds in the very fine photograph shown above.

They spring quickly into action when the order comes

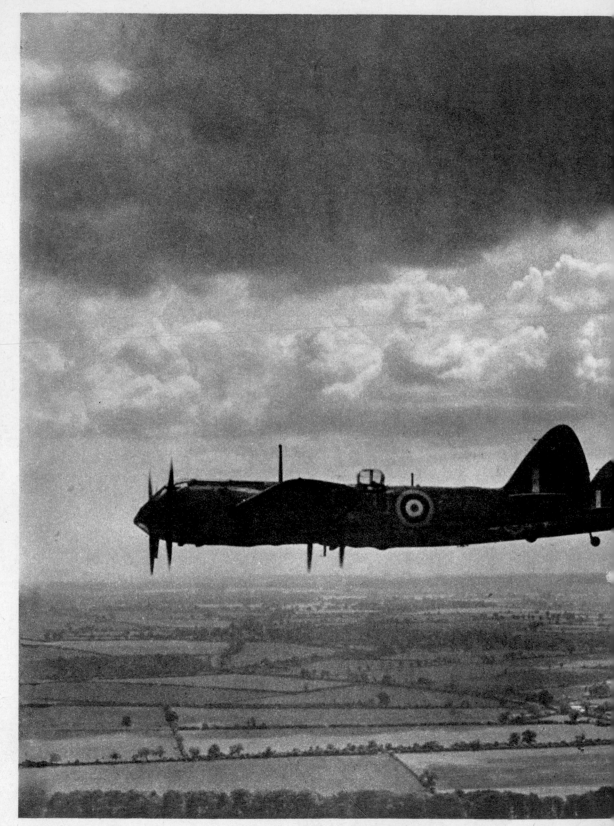

BLENHEIMS—BRITAIN'S FIRST MODER

Grim purpose written in every line, Blenheim bombers wing their way across country towards thei
objective. The Blenheim was the first modern high-speed bomber to be produced for Britain and wa

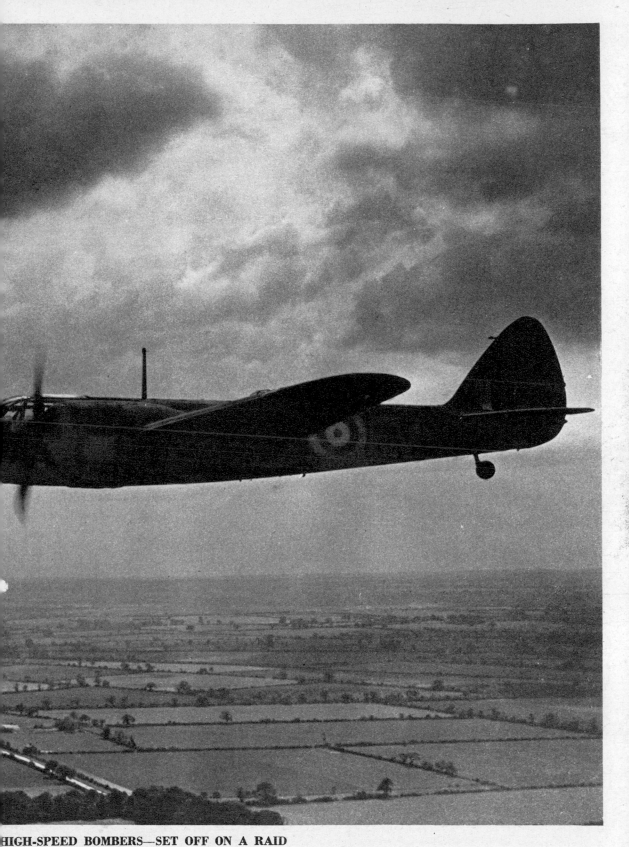

HIGH-SPEED BOMBERS—SET OFF ON A RAID

a useful all-round craft. It took part in almost every type of operation, coastal reconnaissance, attacks on shipping, day and night bombing, day escort fighting and night fighting and proved very satisfactory.

GROWTH OF BOMBER COMMAND

Not so spectacular as the story of the Fighter Command, that of Bomber Command was one of a consistent, long-term, patiently pursued policy in the course of which many million miles were flown. Bombing-up process of loading bombs from low trolleys into internal bays or cells is completed. Carefully "briefed" as to their objective the "Minions of the moon" file towards their craft—pilot, bomb-aimer, navigator, radio operator and gunner-crew, complement varying between three and seven. Less deliberate is the programme of the day bomber, which may take off at short notice, for example to bomb an enemy convoy, just spotted. The illustration opposite shows a crew putting twin machine-guns into a bomber before taking off on a daylight raid.

INSIDE A BOMBER

On the opposite page you see the pilot, top, the second pilot, left, and "Sparks" underneath, lean, serious, concentrated, all at their places in a four-engined Halifax bomber. They are the brains of a giant machine with a wing span of 99 ft., length 70 feet, height 22 feet. Their target may be Germany or Northern Italy. Above, is "the sting in the tail." The air-gunner sits in the bullet-resisting, splinter-proof rear turret of a heavy bomber. During the preparations for a flight, while the bombs were being loaded, tanks filled, oxygen bottles tested, the armourers tested the turret's hydraulic mechanism, the ammunition tanks were filled with long snake-like belts of bullets for the deadly Browning machine-gun. The quickly turning turret supplied the want of mobility in the heavy craft. Placing of the armament varied with the many different and changing forms of aircraft used.

ONE MACHINE—STAFF OF FIFTY-SIX

The personnel needed to service and fly a heavy bomber of the "Stirling" type is seen here, consisting of 1, The Air Crew, which comprises captain, second pilot, air gunner-bomb aimer, flight engineer, observer (navigator), wireless operator and two air gunners. 2, Meteorological Officer. 3, W.A.A.F. parachute packer. 4, Flying control officer.

5, Flight maintenance, (12). 6, Ground servicing, (18). 7, Bombing-up team, numbering 11. 8, Bomber tractor-driver. 9, The starter battery, operated by the flight maintenance crew. 10, Oil bowzer driver. 11, Petrol bowzer driver (corporal) with one A.C.2. Even this team represents but a small percentage of the total number which it is necessary to employ in the upkeep of one large bomber.

FLYING BOATS THAT "SEARCH AND STRIKE"

The Sunderland flying boat, one of the largest aircraft used by the R.A.F., with a speed of 210 miles per hour, a flight duration of 10½ hours, skims gracefully down to the sea. Dwarfed by distance is its great wing span.

CO-OPERATION BY LAND AND SEA

A favourable air situation is necessary for ships and armies to work successfully together. The interrelation of the services indeed was one of the main strategical necessities brought home by the war. It was essential for one thing that aircraft should act as eyes for land and sea forces, thus the camera was the chief weapon of the Army Co-operation Squadron. Above, a camera is being taken into a Lysander Army co-operation plane, about to depart on reconnaissance. In the background the observer gunner is loading ammunition for his machine guns. Visual reconnaissance was also the primary purpose of the flying boats of the Coastal Command, though, to that basis was added a striking power of great effectiveness in the incessant warfare of coast and sea.

NEMESIS OF THE SKIES

Giant sisters were the Stirling, Halifax, and Avro-Lancaster bombers—effective alike in speed, range, and huge bomb load. Instruments of avenging justice, these machines represented a decisive stage in aerial evolution and were the products of large-scale production both in Britain and overseas. Above, are Halifax bombers in flight. The Lancaster shown on the opposite page, had a wing span of 102 feet, length 69 feet, height between 19 and 20 feet, and a maximum speed of about 300 m.p.h. Lancasters left their mark on the submarine yards and slipways of the Baltic coast and in the thousand-bomber raids which brought Nemesis to Germany.

WHILE THE CITY BURNS—AMATEUR FIREMEN SHOW THEIR METTLE

Civil Defence

THE plan of civil defence proved itself a staunch bulwark of British resistance to air attack. Air Raid Precautions (first roughly outlined in 1935) were taken seriously in hand after the September crisis of 1938. As soon as war threatened, air raid wardens and special police went on duty; the auxiliary firemen reported to their stations; the decontamination centres were ready in the event of a gas attack; the hospitals were cleared to receive casualties. Trenches were dug, shelters made, sand-bags piled up, lights obscured, the whole face of Britain was changed overnight. Though some time elapsed before the defences were put to the trial, they were fully equal to it when the trial came. Night fighters, anti-aircraft guns, astonishing secret devices which used wireless rays to detect and record the location of approaching aircraft, ensured that the enemy could never approach unchallenged or unscathed. At the same time it was shown that the care devoted to the organization of the Civil Defence Forces and the great expenditure involved, were entirely justified. Amateur firemen, drawn from many different walks of life, fought the most formidable outbreaks of fire with great courage and skill. Rescue parties behaved with like coolness and promptitude. It was shown that the demoralization of the country by bombing was impossible. The strain of action and loss of sleep was written in every visage during the ferocious bombing attacks made on British cities; but something else was written there too—a realization that the enemy had done his worst, and that it could never prevail. Civil Defence became every man and woman's job. It could never be said that the job was finished though it had its lulls and pauses. Constant vigilance was the watchword of the great host of civilian defenders on the Home Front.

NIGHT SKY PATTERN
The searchlights sweep round the horizon as enemy raiders attempt to penetrate the defences of the city.

PERSONNEL OF CIVIL DEFENCE

The Civil Defence Services, paid and unpaid, numbered just short of a million by June, 1940. In addition, Fire Services accounted for 200,000 persons, Police for 60,000, Casualty personnel for 250,000. From the beginning of war, the "Deep shelter mentality" as Sir John Anderson termed it, was discouraged, though the form of domestic shelter, known to fame as the "Anderson" was distributed on a nation-wide scale, and followed by a type of indoor shelter. As the totalitarian nature of the war became more evident, and bombing was not confined to military objectives, to assist in defence clearly became the duty of all, and every street and district had its fireguard of the able-bodied men and women residents supplementing the trained and specialised services, who were always on duty.

Fireguard with stirrup pump ready.

Fire watchers sign on.

TRAIL OF AIR BATTLE

8.48 a.m., November 17, 1940, was the time and date on which this photograph was taken. The occasion—interception and destruction of a strong force of enemy daylight raiders over the Thames Estuary.

Battle Over Britain

THE story of the great days from August 8th to October 31st, 1940, ranks in British history with the story of the dispersal of the Spanish Armada. In the first phase of the daylight air onslaught on Britain the attack was launched on airfields between London and the coast, beginning with the bombing of coastal cities. This attack failed, and a short lull followed. From August 24th to September 5th the attack was diverted to aerodromes and aircraft factories inland. Again the attack was repulsed with heavy loss. The third stage was the mass attack on London. As it went on the proportion of German losses to British rose higher and higher—the total enemy loss in this phase amounting to 883 aircraft. Decisively beaten, the Germans were then reduced to indiscriminate night-bombing of London and the provincial cities. The Battle of Britain was over, though the Battle over Britain was to continue, and to lay heavy demands on the steadfastness and bravery of the people. As time went on, night bombing, countered with surprising effectiveness by anti-aircraft defences and night fighters, died down, though at no time was the country immune from the stealthy hit and run bomber. The following photographs form a series of vivid impressions of the attack by day and night. They show the ruins of harmless little private houses, of churches and national monuments sacrificed to the vindictive fury of the baffled enemy. They show also how the people bore the trial, and how they won through. Yet through all the violence of destruction, Britain's trains ran, her newspapers were printed, her morning milk was delivered, and the worst devastations of the enemy were set at nought by a mighty host of unknown civilians, who carried on indifferent to danger.

DUEL IN THE AIR

In August, 1940, the people of Britain became spectators of the intense and deadly contests between British fighters and German Heinkels, Dorniers and Messerschmitts. Over Kent and Sussex, Hampshire and Dorset, Essex and London itself, wreathed the patterns of white vapour which were the only leisurely thing about these duels of the air. No single picture can represent the breathless encounter of two hostile aircraft approaching each other at the rate of their combined speeds—six hundred miles an hour—at a height of some five or six miles. The picture above represents the track of battle between a British fighter and five Nazi fighter-bombers, while at right above, is a Spitfire nosing into position for the burst of fire which will bring down its quarry—one of the "Flying Pencils"—Dornier 17s, seen at right, hurtling down in flames.

A raider falls in flames.

An enemy bomber has turned tail, jettisoning its load which falls harmlessly in a meadow.

Messerschmitt fighters, operating singly, made attacks on barrage balloons, one of which is here seen falling in flames over the south-east coast. But these manoeuvres were of little avail, the toll of enemy aircraft daily increased.

GRAVEYARD OF GERMAN HOPES

German airmen landed to become prisoners—German planes piled up on British soil in mounds of scrap metal.

RAIDERS OVER THE HOPFIELDS   In the fields of Kent, the hop pickers many of whom were children, took cover in trenches, and watched with breathless interest the aerial navies' grapple in the blue.

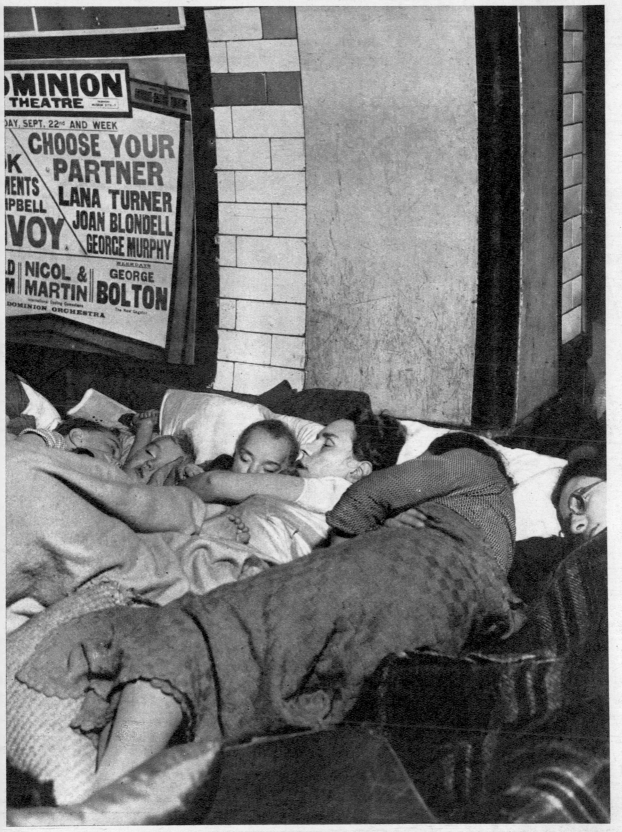

The contrast here is between town and country and also between successive stages of the battles. Town dwellers slept underground when the night raids began in earnest.

AND BY NIGHT
IN THE TOWN

HOW LONDONERS SLEPT IN 1940

In the Air Raid Year as 1940 has been called, shelter life at night became general. Some people stayed where they were, some used basements or cellars, some the Anderson shelters, cold or wet as they might be. But in London large numbers went to the Tube stations —not only for safety but for relief from the tremendous din of gunfire and bombs. The Government had discouraged the making of deep shelters: but the public invaded the Tube stations, and having bought three-halfpenny tickets, claimed the right to spend the nights there—on escalators, platforms or on the line itself. The many existing photographs of scenes of this kind, show huddled groups of civilians, like soldiers trying to find sleep in the front line. At first chaotic, a sort of abnormal order grew out of the new conditions—shelter marshals took charge, neat bunks were fitted up. Over all public shelters inspection was enforced, regulations assuring enough air space to each person made, and proper sanitary arrangements installed. The London Transport Board, with its great faculty for organization, sent food trains to the shelter stations and catered for a quarter of a million people. Though the authorities feared the danger of infection, this period of Home Front activity passed with no unusual epidemic and rather less than the usual incidence of illness. It was a passing phase in any case. The intensity of bombardment dwindled and there came a time during the war when the neat rows of bunks on the stations were already relics of a bygone period. Their function scarcely occurred to the mind of the worker hurrying to catch his train. The fantastic compositions which the cameraman of 1940 recorded, seemed already to belong to another existence of an altogether different kind.

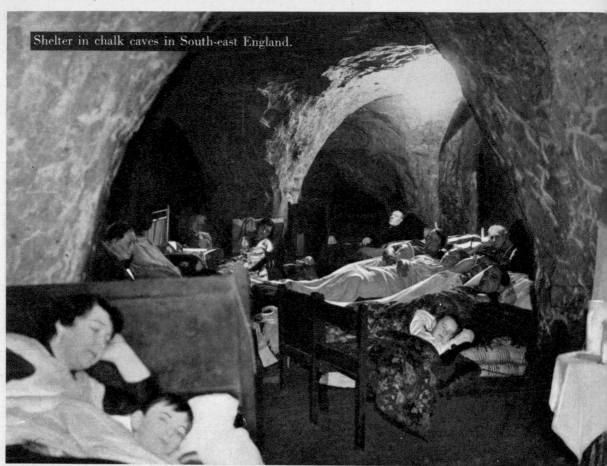

Shelter in chalk caves in South-east England.

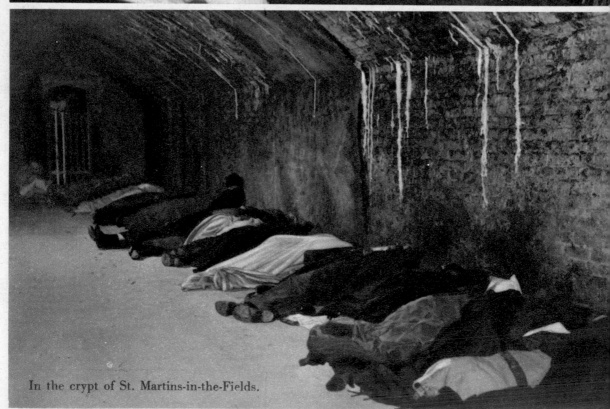

In the crypt of St. Martins-in-the-Fields.

Underground Shelter in East London.

PLACES TO SLEEP

Shelters took varied forms, all with a strange air of unreality. For example, the dwellers in the Southeast, where caves existed in the chalk ridges and cliffs, made their beds, and even transported actual bedsteads to the grottoes, whilst in every department of the Underground Railway system sleepers were to be found, and some for a while found shelter in church crypts, though such temporary shifts were quickly replaced by comfortable quarters, and most of these unusual dormitories were not long occupied.

At a Tube Station

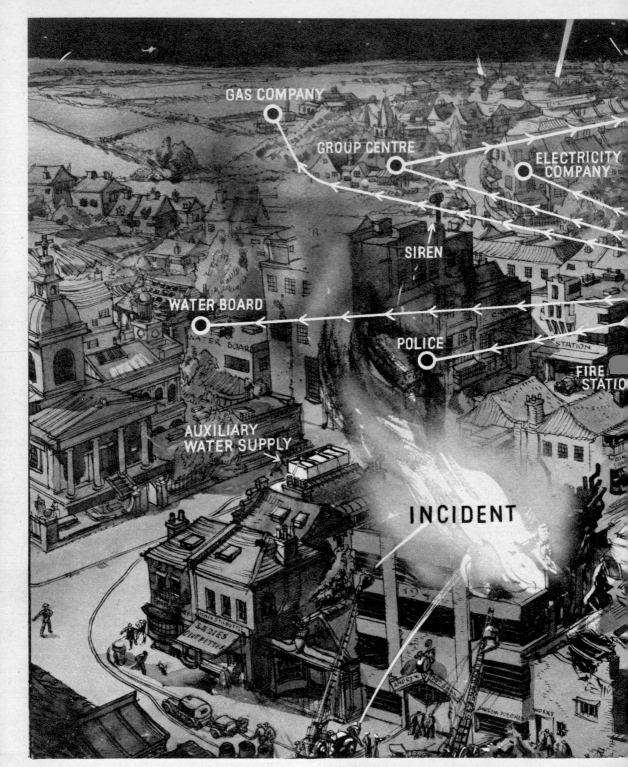

GAS COMPANY

GROUP CENTRE

ELECTRICITY COMPANY

SIREN

WATER BOARD

POLICE

STATION

FIRE STATION

AUXILIARY WATER SUPPLY

INCIDENT

WHAT HAPPENED WHEN THE

How the civil defence services came into action is graphically shown in this picture. A comprehensive system linked up the whole series of operations. The warden observed the incident (represented by the burning building in the foreground) and reported to the Wardens' Post. The Post immediately reported to the Borough Report Centre where officials got in touch with the Police, Fire Force, and A.R.P. Depot where the rescue parties and ambulances were ready to make to the scene. The Fire Force is shown on the spot. The gas, electricity, and water-board headquarters were informed so that they should be ready to disconnect supplies in

Labels within the illustration:

HOME SECURITY
WAR ROOMS

REGIONAL H·Q

BOROUGH
REPORT CENTRE

A·R·P DEPOT
AMBULANCES
RESCUE PARTIES *Etc*

FIRST AID
POST

THE RED LION

FAP

ARP POST

WARDEN OBSERVES
AND REPORTS TO POST

FIRE WATCHERS
ON ROOF

ANDREW DODIE MAN

FIRE BOMBS DROPPED

the event of damage. After the dispatch of services, the Borough Control informed the Group Centre whose job it was to handle inter-borough assistance in cases where the concentration of attack might require equal concentration of units of defence. The Group Centre informed Regional Headquarters, who arranged the distribution of assistance over the group areas. The Regional Headquarters, in turn, kept the Home Security War Rooms informed of the situation within the region. From this main organizing source inter-regional assistance and the whole civil defence policy of the country was conducted. Organization proved itself of real effect.

THEY PLUNGED DEEP INTO THE BELT OF FLAME

The men who joined the Fire Service upheld a tradition as great in its way as the tradition of the Fighting Services—that of Britain's Fire Brigades. Out of 1,400 odd Fire Brigades, with attendant Auxiliary Fire Services, was created a new National Fire Service. The test of the amateur firemen came after months of inactivity, but when it came, it was stupendous in its character. In London it seemed at one time as if the whole city was aflame. The mighty struggle with fire, under bombardment, was continuous and remorseless. The greatest docks in the world burned sporadically for three days. Amid fired buildings, gutters running with blackened water, exploding bombs, billows of choking black smoke, under an inflamed and sinister sky, the firemen fought the flames at the constant peril of their lives, fought with grim persistence, and prevailed. Above, they are seen fighting a blaze in the Commercial Road in the East End of London and at left, in the Temple.

AS THE FIRE RAISERS PASSED OVER

There were many such scenes as this—where London firemen grappled with a fierce outbreak in City warehouses.

HOW THE RESCUE PARTIES TOILED AMONG THE RUINS

The photographs on these pages were taken during the height of the air attack on London. They bring vividly before the eyes the conditions under which the rescue parties worked, stumbling through heaps of debris, toiling with the briefest spells of rest, ignoring all personal danger in the effort to bring out alive the unfortunates trapped under piles of masonry or unconscious in ruinous houses —to recover the bodies of those who were slain.

Few words are needed. These pictures tell their own pitiful story. Here are the civilian **HER HOME** victims of Germany's wanton onslaught. An individual human life is cut suddenly short. **HAS GONE** One is left, stunned and wretched, among the ruins of an innocent, hard-working existence.

HOW THEY "TOOK IT" "We can take it" was the boast of the people of British cities. As air bombing grew in fury, so did their determination. They march proudly with a few salvaged belongings, shouldering a broom like a banner. The good humour of the people is invincible. They can still laugh and joke over mishaps; and play a tune on the piano which now stands in the street.

BLITZ DOG The British love of animals was evidenced many times during air raids. This dog, which was buried for three days, was unearthed by men of the Auxiliary Military Pioneer Corps.

The children have picked up cats which stayed on the site of their former homes and **BLITZ CATS** submit to the caresses of their small protectors with the immovable dignity of their kind.

FANTASY OF WAR Many were the queer and fantastic effects created incidentally in air raids. Here the billiard table leans over at an alarming angle from the upper floor, while beer is served across a counter which might belong to some weird stage set instead of everyday life.

Vehicles achieve a distortion stranger than the imagination of ultra-modern artists ever conceived.

The post-office was non-existent. Telegrams were accepted in the street and written on the backs of messengers.

IN WESTMINSTER ABBEY

The Germans referred to their air attacks on London as a "choir of vengeance." The attempt to wreak this "vengeance" was directed against the most venerated and historic of London's monuments, as well as against the homes of the people. Some damage was done to Westminster Abbey, though fortunately this was slight. Here is the litter-strewn interior of the Abbey after a raid. The statues of great statesmen are untouched

AT THE ALTAR OF ST. PAUL'S

The great Cathedral stood entire though bombs rained round it and it did not remain unscathed. A bomb crashed through the roof of the choir smashing the high altar and injuring the marble reredos. Our photograph is symbolic of the vandalism which seemed to be especially directed against churches, though its savagery failed to achieve that complete and barbarous triumph of destruction which was the perverted ideal of the attackers.

BANQUET IN GIRDLERS' HALL

In stately surroundings the members of this Worshipful and Ancient City Company formerly held their banquets. Now amid the vestiges of magnificence workmen have a banquet of their own. The parody of ancient state is unconscious. The ruin is due not to the hand of time but the hand of man. This is one of the historic buildings that had survived the centuries but were wrecked by enemy action against London—like the Guildhall itself, Stationers' Hall and Middle Temple Hall, where Shakespeare's *Twelfth Night* was originally performed.

HISTORY UNDER FIRE

The legendary giants of the City of London, Gog and Magog, were buried beneath a mound of rubble when the Guildhall was set on fire by incendiary bombs in December, 1940. The statue of the giant of literature, Dr. Samuel Johnson, remains looking along the Fleet Street whence he so seldom wandered: though the Church of St. Clement Danes where he often worshipped in his lifetime and in whose churchyard he stands, is but a pathetic shell. Not far away, in the Temple, the friend of the great lexicographer, Oliver Goldsmith, is calmly recumbent and undamaged except for a chip off the nose. The equable philosophy of the eighteenth century seems to come to the aid of these men of letters under conditions of which they never dreamed in their lifetime. In the Great Hall of the Inner Temple (in the left-hand photograph) a statue, reminiscent of mediaeval chivalry, still stands, a knight whom bombing has not reduced to dust. History had come under fire as a new chapter of history was written.

AFTER THE RAID OF DECEMBER 29, 1940 —
A VIEW FROM ST. PAUL'S

DAMAGE AT WESTMINSTER Symbolic also is this photograph. The Dean of Westminster surveys the charred beams, the empty window frames, the scorched and blistered walls of the Deanery—once the finest mediæval house in London, formerly the residence of the pre-Reformation Abbots.

Like many of the minor masterpieces of Sir Christopher Wren, St. Clement's, with its steeple by Gibbs and pulpit by Grinling Gibbons, was ravaged by air attack. The vicar, who died shortly after the raid, lies in state in the ruined building. Uniformed mourners keep vigil.

IN ST. CLEMENT DANES

COVENTRY'S ORDEAL

On the night of November 14th-15th, 1940, in bright moonlight, the German bombers flew over the Midland city of Coventry in waves, dropping over 450 tons of incendiary and high explosive bombs. Widespread destruction was caused. Whole districts were reduced to ruins. 200 people were killed, 800 injured, 35,000 were rendered homeless. The fourteenth-century cathedral was gutted. Fires threatening the whole city were checked only by dynamite. A sad spectacle of devastation met the eyes of the inhabitants on the following morning. The Nazis invented a name for their work—to "Coventrate." If they had thought, however, that by such means they would break the spirit of the British people they were much in error. The city was stricken, but its spirit was unbroken. Its work went on. Temporary buildings sprang up. Plans were made for a new and finer city. Coventry was a type of every British city. Bristol, Portsmouth, Southampton, Birmingham, Liverpool, Manchester, and many other centres suffered much. The list of cities attacked was a long one. The amount of damage done might vary, but the reaction of each was the same, to all equally is praise for their fortitude and courage in the trial.

REMAINS OF COVENTRY'S FOURTEENTH-CENTURY CATHEDRAL

THE TEMPLE IN PEACE AND WAR

A city within a city, and an oasis of quiet from the roar of Fleet Street and the Strand, the Temple has been an especial pride of Londoners. Since the days when the Knights Templars in the twelfth century purchased the stretch of land between Fleet Street and the Thames, it has grown with each age, its architecture and associations being continually enriched. The mellow buildings, the stone-flagged pavement, the quiet charm typical of this home of lawyers are seen on this page as they were. It remained for war to shatter the mellow bricks and stone, to blow out the windows, and to produce the battered travesty of the Temple's former self seen opposite.

PUMP COURT, TEMPLE (OPPOSITE) BEFORE AND (ABOVE) AFTER THE RAIDS

BUCKINGHAM PALACE

ST. JAMES'S PALACE

**LONDON'S FAMOUS
CARLTON HOUSE TERRACE**

THE LITTLE HOMES OF BRITAIN

Rich and poor, great and small suffered equally from indiscriminate bombing.

Damage at Canterbury.

The wrecked Cathedral Library.

Interior of Exeter Cathedral.

GUIDE-BOOK

The so-called "Baedeker" raids on Britain were made by Germany in 1942 as a reprisal for the bombing of Cologne and other industrial centres. The avowed aim was to destroy towns and buildings of historical beauty. In pursuit of this ideal the Nazis in spiteful fury, struck at York, Bath, Canterbury, Exeter, and Norwich.

Ruined cloisters of Exeter.

Bath, with the damaged St. Andrew's Church

The fired Guildhall, York.

VANDALISM

Some damage was done, as may be seen from the photographs on these pages. The Guildhall at York was gutted, the Cathedral at Exeter was damaged, the beautiful streets of Bath were scarred, many relics of ancient England were destroyed at Canterbury. Palpably none of these buildings had military or industrial importance.

AFTER THE RAIDS— CLEARING UP

A hundred different problems were left in the wake of intensive bombing. Unsafe buildings must be pulled down and the Auxiliary Pioneer Corps put their backs into this part of the job as may be seen in this photograph, where an unsafe wall is being brought to the ground. Unexploded bombs were another menace, and many quiet feats of heroism were performed by the "Suicide Squad," whose task it was to dig out and render harmless the potentially deadly projectiles. A time bomb which threatened St. Paul's and, if it had exploded, would have infallibly done great damage to the fabric, was excavated at the risk of their lives by one such squad. The bomb was taken to the Hackney Marshes and there disposed of without harm. Demolition workers were silhouetted against the city skies as they applied their pick-axes to the shaky brickwork of tall buildings damaged in raids, and neatly constructed tanks of "static water" appeared on the cleared sites. So well was the work of clearing up done that the cities of Britain quickly resumed their trim aspect, though the scars of bombing were not to be entirely effaced and might even receive additions. In many places such scars were a constant reminder of the work of planning and reconstruction that remained to be done in the future.

MR. CHURCHILL SURVEYS THE DAMAGED HOUSE OF COMMONS

THE PRIME MINISTER ON THE AIR WAR

"Herr Hitler declared on September 4th (1940) that as we would not bend to his will, he would wipe out our cities. I have no doubt that when he gave the order he sincerely believed that it was in his power to carry his will into effect. However, the cities of Britain are still standing. They are quite distinctive objects in the landscape and our people are going about their tasks with the utmost activity."

". . . the bearing of our people not only in London, but in Birmingham, Liverpool, Manchester and other places, has gained the unstinted admiration of all classes throughout the British Empire, throughout the United States and, as far as they have been allowed to hear about it, among the peoples of the captive countries. Surveying the whole scene, alike in its splendour and devastation, I see no reason to regret that Herr Hitler tried to break the British spirit by the blind bombing of our cities and countryside."

(Extracts from speech by Mr. Churchill in the House of Commons, November 5, 1940.)

The workers cheer the Prime Minister as he tours the City of Plymouth after heavy raids.

WHEN INVASION THREATENED—GUARDS AT THE ADMIRALTY

Preparing for Invasion

WHEN the resistance of France collapsed and the British Expeditionary Force was evacuated from Dunkirk, the invasion of Britain became a very real menace.

The nation had long rested in a sense of security. Her reliance on the protection afforded by the sea had been implicit. Now, as in the Napoleonic days, the coasts must be manned. Watch and ward against assaults by airborne troops must be kept.

An immediate sign of these preparations was the disappearance of anything that might guide an invader on his arrival. Gangs of men were seen removing road signs, painting out place-names on public buildings, hoardings and placards. Travellers by train were disconcerted by the anonymity of the stations through which they passed. Ways to the sea were barred, and those who, for sufficient reason, were allowed access to coastal areas were enjoined to walk warily. Great ditches and tank traps ran like scars across the face of the countryside. Huge concrete barriers straddled the main highways at strategic points. Government offices and other important public buildings were screened with barbed wire entanglements, through which all visitors had to pick their way under the eye of armed sentries.

The people of Britain had realised their danger. They moved spontaneously to the protection of the land. They demanded and got a civilian army. Workers who could not be spared for the regular forces, and those who were too old for active service, were enrolled for home defence.

E

WHERE THE ARMY GUARDS THE NARROW SEAS—A CIRCULAR SEA FORT

At first, they had neither uniforms nor weapons. They drilled in their shirt-sleeves at the end of the day's work. They route-marched on Sundays and half-holidays, using sticks for rifle drill, and stones as practice grenades.

Others, men and women, became coast watchers, or stood on guard beside the silent bells of churches, ready to peal the alarm at sight of enemy parachute troops. Yet others formed emergency first-aid and medical services, or organized local arrangements to maintain essential services against any contingency that might cut off their neighbourhood from the normal means of communication.

The immediate crisis of invasion passed, but the civilian army, the Home Guard, remained, perfecting its training: well knowing that the enemy waited for vigilance to be relaxed; and determined to play its part with the efficiency required by modern warfare.

WATCH ON THE COAST

Key points in the fixed defences on the southern coast of Britain were forts of steel and concrete in the sea itself. Their garrisons of artillery were ready for instant action by day or night and each was crammed with guns and munitions. Every possible landing-place was covered by fire-power and the coast was lined with guns of every calibre. A heavy coastal gun with its pattern of camouflage is seen in action in the above photograph. If the would-be invader had tried to keep to the schedule arrogantly planned, he would have met with a hot reception.

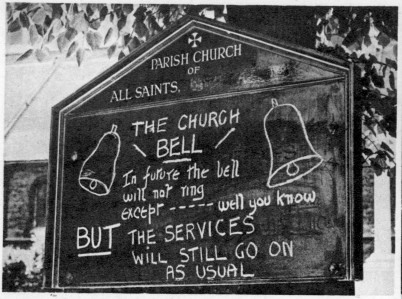

"IF THE INVADER COMES"

While, in 1940, Goering (like Napoleon) paced the sands of Boulogne, looking across the sea towards Britain; while English phrase books were being doled out to the Nazi troops and the barges waited in readiness, from Brest to Rotterdam; at home, in Britain, sweeping preparations were in progress. An official leaflet in plain, blunt type was received in every home: "If the Invader Comes—What to do and How to do it." As the individual prepared to do his or her part, a general order brought a strange anonymity to the land. Road signs, milestones, names of railway stations, all hints of direction were whisked out of sight. The church bells were silenced. Obstacles of many kinds appeared on the roads—blockhouses, barbed wire entanglements, machine-gun nests, anti-tank traps. Highways and country lanes alike bristled with tanks and guns. So effective was the clearance of signs that the inhabitants found it no easy matter to get from place to place, and no stranger could avoid a sharp scrutiny.

HOME GUARD IN TRAINING

In July, 1940, it was announced that the volunteers for military defence at home numbered more than 1,300,00 men. There could be no more conclusive proof of the fighting spirit of the country. Willingness outra equipment—and training was carried on at the beginning with makeshift weapons and in plain clothes. Th story of this civilian force is a triumph of national enthusiasm. From the original band of Local Defen Volunteers, poorly equipped and sketchily organized, there grew a smart, well-disciplined army, trained in th special technique that its position as auxiliary to the Regular Army required. Speed, mobility, fieldcraft (streetcraft) and fire power have been defined as the four essentials of this technique. Local knowledge wou obviously count for much, and the photographs on these pages show some of the "battles" that provided valuab experience. Above is an encounter at close quarters in a suburb of a North of England town. The steel helme represent the enemy paratroops engaged by the defending force. The combatants were miners of the distri

Home Guards and Canadian troops both take part in a street-fighting exercise.

Holding-up the enemy—an "invasion" scene in the City of London.

THE HOME GUARD IS READY
Along the cliff edge winds a file of alert
uniformed men going to their posts.

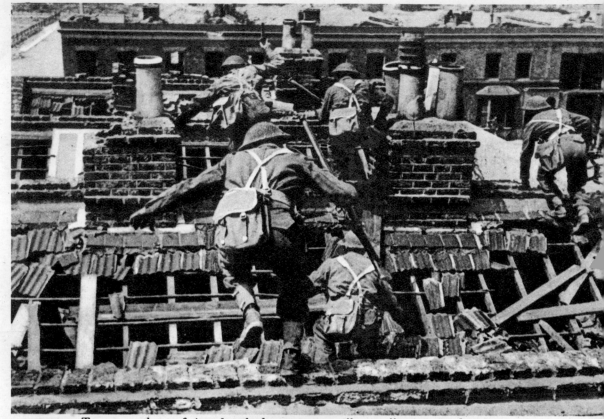

Troops on the roofs in a bombed area mop up "enemy" snipers and strong points.

Home Guards prepare to deal with an " invader " by means of Molotov cocktails.

Royal Horse Artillery in action during a mock invasion.

Home Guards rush a village under cover of a smoke bomb.

WHICH SHOW SHALL WE GO TO?

This picture of wartime theatreland tells its own story. Out of the fifty theatres and music halls under the juris-
diction of the London County Council the great majority applied for the renewal of their licences and carried on

Lunch-time concert at the National Gallery.

Diversions

THE war produced some notable changes in the methods adopted by the British People to employ their limited leisure. Theatres and cinemas were, of course, as popular as ever. The lighter side of entertainment suffered no priggish disapproval, but an enormous interest began to be shown in many things of value which large numbers of people had never much bothered about in peace-time. It would be putting it crudely to say that the people became, suddenly, music lovers, book readers, connoisseurs of the arts : there is no doubt however, that they took quite sincerely and unaffectedly to these modes of diversion. The appearance on exhibition of a single chosen picture from the national collection produced an eager crowd of visitors. The concerts at the National Gallery became an institution and the revived "Proms." at the Albert Hall were hugely attended. Books, technical, historical, classical, were read with a new eagerness. Various bodies, among which the Council for the Encouragement of Music and the Arts should be mentioned, helped to foster this development. At the same time the British People, as always, sang comic songs and enjoyed listening to them: danced—and were stimulated by Transatlantic visitors to become knowledgeable about baseball.

SERIOUS PLEASURES

There was a call from people in every kind of wartime occupation for serious books, and a general desire to read, to appreciate good things, and discuss serious questions. The "Brains Trust," one of the successes of wartime broadcasting claimed the interest of some six million listeners who wished to know the meaning of love, the origin of arithmetic, and other deep matters. The questions were answered spontaneously and a session is seen in progress above, including (from left to right) Philip Guedalla, Professor Julian Huxley, Ritchie Calder, C. E. M. Joad, Commander Campbell and the "question-master," D. S. McCullough. At left, students in uniform spend their off-duty time at a bookshop.

NON-STOP THEATRE OF THE AIR RAIDS

Throughout the blitz period one little theatre distinguished itself by keeping going its continuous variety entertainment. The performers slept in the theatre itself which provided both stage and shelter. Above, is a performance at the Windmill Theatre with a nautical chorus and an appropriate backcloth, if not the most serious type of costume. At right is a photograph actually taken during a raid, of the show girls asleep behind the scenes. The discipline of the footlights, implicit in the phrase "The show must go on" was well demonstrated during the war.

WORKERS' PLAYTIME

On these pages are some aspects of wartime amusement and recreation. ENSA—Entertainments National Service Association was an official body, which provided concerts for the forces and factory workers and for which stage and music hall performers freely gave their services. Above, Mr. George Formby, junior, raises a laugh from a factory audience at one of these concerts which were held in many different parts of Britain.

Land girls and men of the Merchant Navy enjoy a dance.

Baseball fascinates a large audience at Wembley Stadium.

RUSSIA COMES TO WARTIME BRITAIN

A new interest in things Russian was the result of the admiration felt in Britain for the gallant resistance of their partners in the cause of the United Nations. The U.S.S.R. had shown itself not only heroic in war, but capable in organisation, and enlightened in ideas: and the expressions of Soviet culture found an appreciative audience. Russian Ballet it is true had long been a staple attraction to the British theatregoer. Now it was also a spiritual link with an Ally. Many were mindful that when the Germans were at the gates of Moscow in 1941, the opera and ballet went on, and the fact that they did so encouraged the defenders of the city to renewed exertions. Thus Britain welcomed with more than usual acclaim the wave of Russian or Russia inspired stage productions in 1942. Of these "Sorochintsi Fair" and the new ballet "The Great Gates of Kieff," a scene from which is here illustrated, were outstanding. Incidentally, an Anglo-Polish ballet company was formed to tour those places in Great Britain where Polish troops were billeted and this also was the object of much interest, eventually settling down to a season in London. The wartime vogue of ballet was even reflected in an adapted version of *Hamlet*.

CINEMA IN WARTIME

The war naturally brought with it some change in the subject and style of film production, though it is worthy of note that one outstanding pre-war success "Gone with the Wind" remained a popular favourite. There was a crop of war stories of varying merit; and some serious efforts to represent the events of the period as they affected the average man and woman—events which almost seemed to defy the attempts of screen narrative to be anything but trivial by comparison. Of these efforts "Mrs. Miniver" was considered to be a very satisfactory rendering of the drama of real life on the British "home front." The exciting possibilities of a Continental background were utilised in "One of Our Aircraft is Missing."

"MRS. MINIVER"

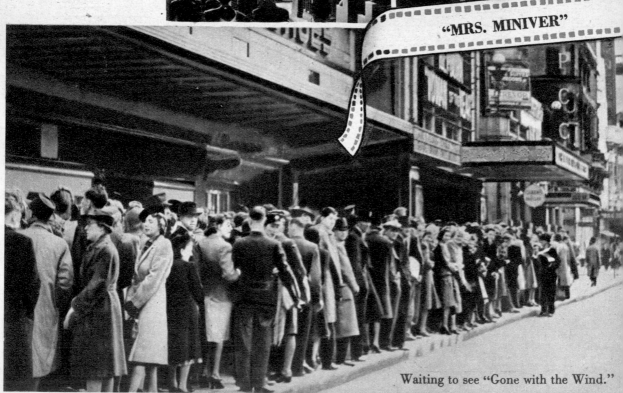

Waiting to see "Gone with the Wind."

"ONE OF OUR AIRCRAFT IS MISSING"

SCENES FROM THE FILMS

"Mrs. Miniver" depicted the lives of an English middle-class family during war. The stills from it on the opposite page show the family in their Anderson shelter: Mrs. Miniver and the German airman who has sought refuge: and service in the bombed church. The scenes at left on this page from "One of Our Aircraft is Missing" show the airmen getting their orders for the night's operations and scenes of escape from Holland.

Then and Now

THE mirrors of peace and war are placed side by side, reflecting, in a double image, the enormous change that has come over life in Britain. Pomp and pageantry give place to battledress, the shining cuirass of the Lifeguard is replaced by plain khaki, the antique splendour of the Lord Mayor's Show turns into a military march. The tank has ousted the pleasure car from the mainroad, the shooting season has begun in real earnest, the beauty chorus "shows a leg" in the A.T.S., and the child of the pavements is learning about rural life. Going back in the past somewhat further than just pre-war—about a quarter of a century when another war was on—there is a difference without a distinction. Then, also the women worked on the land and in factories, though hairdressers had another style, skirts were very long indeed and the girls at the machines were called "munitionettes." The swings and roundabouts of Hampstead Heath on a Bank Holiday are the same now as ever, but with this difference—that American soldiers are here to sample the fun and their companions wear utility fashions. In these and other signs of the times the evolution of a country is clearly written.

PROCESSION—1938
Lord Mayor's Show

LAND GIRLS 1918

LAND GIRLS 1942

WOMEN AT WAR 1918

WOMEN AT WAR 1942

A·B·C·D
OVERSEAS SHORTWAVE BANDS TO
ALL PARTS OF THE WORLD FORM A
CONTINUOUS WORLD SERVICE
THROUGHOUT THE 24 HOURS

HOW BRITAIN BROADCAST TO

The voice of Britain could be heard in every part of the globe, bringing reassurance and hope to the occupied territories and counteracting the insidious propaganda of the enemy. The extent of this activity which had the collaboration of free nationals of various lands may be gathered from this diagram. It formed a continuous

DAILY TRANSMISSIONS TO EUROPEAN COUNTRIES

KEY TO WORLD MAP

A·ICELAND B·SPAIN & PORTUGAL
C·FRANCE D·CORSICA & SARDINIA
E·MALTA F·SWITZERLAND G·ITALY H·GREECE I·ALBANIA J·BELGIUM
K·YUGOSLAVIA L·CYPRUS M·TURKEY N·BULGARIA O·AUSTRIA P·HUNGARY
Q·RUMANIA R·CZECHO-SLOVAKIA S·HOLLAND T·GERMANY U·POLAND
V·DENMARK W·FINLAND X·SWEDEN Y·NORWAY

1 ICELANDIC & ENGLISH
2 FRENCH & ENGLISH
3 ENGLISH
4 FRENCH & ENGLISH
5
6 PORTUGUESE SPANISH & ENGLISH
7
8 FRENCH, MOROCCAN ARABIC & ENGLISH
9 DUTCH, AFRIKAANS PORTUGUESE SPANISH & ENGLISH
10 PORTUGUESE & ENGLISH
11 FRENCH & ENGLISH
12 LOCAL LANGUAGES & ENGLISH
13 FRENCH, PERSIAN ARABIC & ENGLISH
14 LOCAL LANGUAGES & ENGLISH
15 DUTCH
16 ENGLISH
17 FRENCH
18 ENGLISH
19 ENGLISH
20 LOCAL LANGUAGES & ENGLISH
21 NORWEGIAN & ENGLISH
22 FINNISH & ENGLISH
23 SWEDISH & ENGLISH

THE WHOLE OF THE WORLD

service throughout the twenty-four hours, not only in English, but in all the varieties of world speech from Icelandic to Persian and including the many local languages of the East. Our illustration shows both the overseas shortwave bands to all parts of the world and, inset, the daily transmissions to European countries.

REAPERS ON ONCE DERELICT AREAS OF THE SUSSEX DOWNS

Lord Woolton, Minister of Food, inspects communal cookery.

The Nation's Larder

WHEN war began it was foreseen that imports of foodstuffs must be regulated, to ensure that only essentials were received and stored, and that the unexploited resources of the land itself had to be brought into use. Much more food must be grown at home, and what was grown must be of the highest nutritional value.

Careful surveys were made by expert agriculturalists. They charted the vast tracts of arable land that were unused, and plans were made to bring it under intensive cultivation; whilst scientific methods were introduced to increase the yield of lands already being farmed.

Parklands, commons and downs were converted into great cornfields. Essential foods were cultivated where, hitherto, flowers and luxury fruits had been grown. The nation's resources were mobilized. Farmers were helped and encouraged to grow what was needed. A Land Army of women was formed to replace farm workers called up for military service. Municipalities and rural councils were urged to undertake the cultivation of public lands. Private citizens turned their flower gardens into vegetable-beds; and those who had no gardens were given allotments where enough could be grown to make their households almost self-supporting in vegetable foods.

Meanwhile, the individual was gently but firmly persuaded to regulate his diet according to the availability of the various kinds of food, by the introduction of Ration Cards, which limited the amount each individual might purchase over a given period, of all essential commodities.

Perhaps the average citizen did not always realize what was happening to the foods his ration card prevented him from buying. He did not see the vast dumps, hangars and cold-storage places, where thousands of tons of tinned and otherwise preserved foods were stored against the future. Restrictions were imposed so gradually that he did not appreciate with what resource and benevolent guile the authorities were accustoming him to a plain and wholesome diet, nor with what foresight they were conserving available supplies of the foods which must, perforce, be brought into the country by sea.

At all hazards, vast quantities of supplies had to come that way; and the Lease-Lend arrangement with the U.S.A. had the effect of making that country a main source of provision for those commodities, essential to health, which Britain could not produce at home.

The limitation of shipping space stimulated the inventiveness of those responsible for keeping the people fed. Imported meats were de-boned and de-hydrated before they were shipped; milk and eggs were dried and powdered; essential fruit vitamins were extracted and compressed from the raw pulp in colonial orchards; ingenuity was strained to the limit so that the very maximum amount of nutrition could be carried in minimum space.

Meanwhile, for those who worked at a distance from their homes, communal restaurants were provided, where carefully chosen, well cooked foods were obtainable at low prices; and a great organization was established to extend this communal feeding system to the whole nation in an emergency.

INTENSIVE CULTIVATION. Night ploughing in progress.

DIGGING FOR VICTORY

Allotments were one of the popular legacies of the war 1914-1918. Their number was greatly increased when war again broke out and people were encouraged to produce what they could in their gardens and small plots of ground. *Dig for Victory* was one of the slogans of the time, and a very substantial contribution towards the self-supporting ideal—in vegetable produce at least—was made in this way. Above is an allotment scene at Ilford.

FOOD CONVOY IN ACTION

Plans were made for food supply in emergency and after the concentrated raid on Coventry, "Queen's Messenger" cars, gifts to Britain from the Queen and from America, were at once dispatched to supply the immediate wants of the hungry. The convoy is here seen drawn up for dispersal after it had arrived in the distressed city.

COMMUNAL EATING

Luxury eating, in restaurants during the war was frowned upon and in 1942 a maximum price of five shillings was fixed for a restaurant meal. At the same time a type of communal restaurant approved by the Ministry, where good and inexpensive meals could be had, was being developed. Hundreds of British Restaurants, as they were called, were started in towns all over the country. One is illustrated here. Those first established were somewhat rough and ready, but improvements in decoration and surroundings were made as the plan was developed.

City workers in London have a lunch-time meal supplied by a Queen's Messenger convoy.

DATE	BACON & HAM	SUGAR	BUTTER	COOKING FATS	MEAT	TEA	CHEESE	PRESERVES (MONTH)	POINTS RATIONS (MONTH)
1940 JAN. 8	4 OZ.	12 OZ.	4 OZ.						
1940 JULY 22	4 OZ.	8 OZ.	AND MARGARINE 6 OZ.	2 OZ.	1'10	2 OZ.			
1941 MAY 5	4 OZ.	8 OZ.	6 OZ.	2 OZ.	1/.	2 OZ.	1 OZ.	8 OZ.	
1941 DEC. 1	4 OZ.	12 OZ.	7 OZ.	3 OZ.	1'2	2 OZ.	3 OZ.	1 LB.	16 POINTS
1942 FEB. 23	4 OZ.	8 OZ.	6 OZ.	2 OZ.	1'2	2 OZ.	3 OZ.	1 LB.	20 POINTS

MILK AND EGGS:
(PROPORTION ONLY, EXACT QUANTITIES VARYING)

ASSUMED ADULT ENTITLEMENT ➤ 3 PINTS OF MILK A WEEK   3 EGGS A MONTH

SPECIAL SUPPLIES: MILK —				
EXPECTANT MOTHERS: 7 PINTS	INFANTS: 14 PINTS	CHILDREN: 3½ TO 7 PINTS	INVALIDS: UP TO 14 PINTS	12 EGGS A MONTH FOR CHILDREN AND EXPECTANT MOTHERS

OTHER EXTRAS FOR CHILDREN:

ORANGES   FRUIT JUICE CHILDREN UP TO TWO YEARS   COD LIVER OIL CHILDREN UP TO SIX YEARS

VIDI

HOW RATIONING DEVELOPED IN THREE YEARS OF WAR

Much attention has been given in modern times to the scientific estimate of diet and the problem of rationing, inevitable in wartime was approached not simply as a matter of withholding food but also as of aiming at a correct balance, without waste or excess, of essential elements—calories (or heat and energy units), the proteins (body-building elements) and vitamins (organic compounds essential in small amounts to general health). Carefully devised in this respect and gradually applied was the scheme of rationing organized by the Ministry of Food. The first issue of ration books was based on the National Registration of October 1939 and the system was extended as the above diagram indicates, though bread remained an unrationed staple. The flexible nature of the control over certain commodities, for example milk and eggs, made allowance for the special needs of children and others. It was the policy of the Ministry of Food to provide the maximum ration for all consumers; but a deviation was made in the case of cheese, a special ration being allowed to miners, farm workers and others who could not take their mid-day meal at home. Under the Points scheme whereby the consumer did not register but could spend coupons at any shops, the points were allotted according to the supply position and adjusted according to demand. Catering establishments were tied to a supplier and bought their supplies on the basis of an allowance for each meal served. About 1,500 local Food Control Committees administered the scheme locally. The diagram is based on representative dates in the development of rationing. The high standard of the nation's health in wartime was often remarked. Much criticism was aroused, however, by the activities of food speculators. Lord Woolton warned the food gamblers and price-fixing orders and increasing penalties kept them in check. The Ministry of Food became the "largest trading organization in the world," regulating prices and distribution, and purchasing 90 per cent. of the import of human and animal food.

AUSTERITY WAS THE WATCHWORD OF SOCIAL OCCASIONS

The profusion of banquets was spontaneously reduced. Our photograph shows Rotarians at an "austerity" lunch of which the items were—vegetable soup, pressed meat sandwiches, national bread—and short speeches.

BRITISH AGRICULTURE IN WAR

Agriculture at the beginning of the war was in a much worse and more enfeebled state than it was in 1914. The area under the plough had decreased by 4½ million acres, while at the same time there were some six million more people to feed. The first step was a ploughing-up campaign, involving millions of acres. It was also necessary to increase the yield per acre by the scientific use of fertilizers and to ensure that the maximum amount of grain went into the flour. Ploughing-up was carried out with so much success that in 1942 the Minister of Agriculture was able to report that Britain had covered about two-thirds of the way towards self-sufficiency. Production of all grain over pre-war was increased by two-thirds, potato production by two-thirds, fresh vegetable production by more than 50 per cent. A problem arising out of the ploughing-up of grass land, was the loss of food for animals (also aggravated by the shortage of imported feeding-stuffs), in spite of what the arable crops provided. Loss was partly made good by improving remaining grassland.

The whole family turns out to gather the wartime harvest on this farm in the Lake District.

Women's land army brings in the flax crop—growing in forty times the pre-war quantity.

FERTILE BRITAIN

The bounteous harvests of the war period, of which this photograph gives some suggestion, exceeded all expectations.

Land girls gather in the sugar-beet harvest which supplies Britain's sugar ration.

Police keep a wartime piggery. Pig clubs help to solve the problems of feeding-stuffs.

BRITAIN BUYS THE EMPIRE'S SURPLUS

Nearly 90 per cent. of the country's imports of human and animal food were purchased by the Ministry of Food —the world's greatest purchaser of international foodstuffs. In normal times Britain took nearly the whole of the world's chilled and frozen meat export. During the war it absorbed all the surplus that the Dominions and Colonies could provide, and vast transactions proceeded with astonishing regularity and smoothness. Our photograph shows a cargo of mutton from New Zealand being unloaded at a British port. The gun mounted aft on the ship is a reminder of the perils by sea successfully overcome to bring Britain food from overseas.

FAMOUS LANDMARKS USED TO ENCOURAGE WAR SAVINGS

The sandbagged pyramid which encloses the statute of Eros at Piccadilly Circus displays a series of posters exhorting the people to buy National War Bonds. On the plinth of the Nelson Column, used for such purposes only in times of war or national danger, is a similar call to save for the national good. The response was universal.

Financing the War

O NLY a very few experts, who perform prodigious feats of mathematical ingenuity with astronomical figures running into hundreds of millions of pounds sterling, can work out in detail how wars are paid for. One thing is clear, however, to all. The community must pay, in cash, in goods, and in production.

Britain applied without delay the lessons of 1914-1918 in financing the war. Increased taxation, direct and indirect, was obviously necessary. At the same time, measures of control were imposed to prevent the price of necessities soaring and to prevent profiteering in all its forms.

The art of advertising was used by the Government to impress upon the people the need for saving, and to encourage them to invest their money in ways that would directly augment the nation's war effort. Press and poster advertising alike took on a new and more earnest aspect. Commercial firms used space in a responsible fashion for the national good. Special "Savings Weeks" were organized, and communities competed with one another in providing the biggest totals.

Of several voluntary schemes on behalf of wartime services an amazing example was the Red Cross Penny-a-week Fund, through which millions of pounds were obtained for this great humanitarian cause by regular weekly contributions of a penny.

The solvency of a nation depends not only on its capital resources, but also on the energy with which it conserves its material wealth. So, among the major war-time enterprises of Britain was salvage. The nation cut to the minimum its expenditure, even on the necessities of life. It reclaimed its scraps of food, paper, cloth, metal, and every kind of re-usable material.

A planned system of national economy took shape against the individual background. To conserve man-power, the public services were curtailed, and unnecessary private enterprise was stopped. Passenger train services were reduced to make room for military rail traffic. Petrol was rationed strictly, and motoring was discouraged almost to the point of prohibition. People accustomed themselves to spending their holidays at home.

An interesting device of war-time economy was the introduction of a Government scheme to ensure that no waste of material for clothing occurred through the vagaries of fashion. Designers were officially commissioned to create economical styles of clothing. To the surprise and pleasure of the public, many people were able to obtain well cut, reliable clothes at lower prices than most of them had hitherto been able to afford.

Never before in the history of Britain was wealth so carefully conserved; never were the problems of production and distribution so boldly tackled.

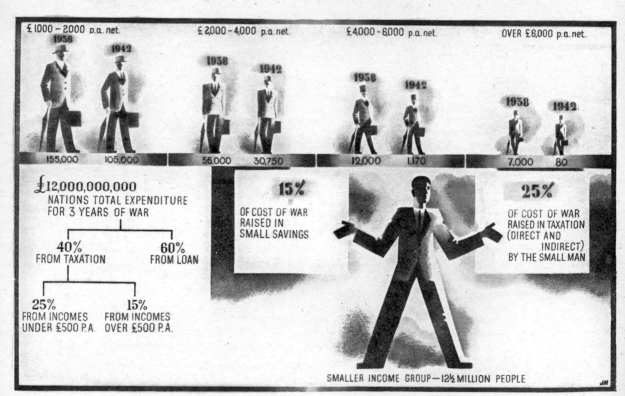

NATIONAL INCOME AND EXPENDITURE IN THREE YEARS OF WAR

This diagram shows graphically the heavy incidence of taxation on large incomes and the contribution of the small man in savings and in taxation direct and indirect, towards the cost of war which by 1942 was averaging £12,000,000 a day. The "smaller income group" comprises all those with incomes of up to £500 a year.

APPORTIONING THE LOAD

The Budget of April, 1941, brought war finance into full operation with Income Tax at 10s. in the £ and surtax at a level where "to enjoy a tax-free income of £5,000 a year, it would be necessary to have a gross income of £66,000 a year." The Budget speech of the Chancellor of the Exchequer, Sir Kingsley Wood, seen at right, was considered to have made finance intelligible to the plain man for the first time. "The financial front since the beginning of the war," he said, "has stood firm and strong." He explained the steps taken to mobilize international purchasing power: to register and requisition foreign securities held by British citizens abroad: He then dealt with the diversion of investment at home to Government issues and the means taken to reduce the post-war burden by borrowing at a low rate of interest. An important development of policy was the control of prices and the prevention of inflation. A welcome sign of national earnestness was the prompt and record yield of Income Tax.

AT THE MANSION HOUSE DURING WARSHIP WEEK

The War Savings Campaign began in November, 1939. It was stimulated by special national efforts such as War Weapons Weeks and Warships Weeks, exhibitions and films. Warships Weeks, held between October 1941 and March 1942 in 1200 savings areas produced about £400 millions. London raised nearly £150 millions. The National Savings Committee under the presidency of Lord Kindersley spurred on the public to amazing results.

SCHOOLCHILDREN HELPED TO SAVE

The younger ones helped. These children organized a dog show, bought Savings Certificates with the proceeds.

SAVINGS AND SALVAGE DOWN OUR STREET

The cheerful people shown above ran a combined streets savings group and salvage collection club.

MATERIAL, AS WELL AS MONEY, WAS PART OF THE SAVINGS CAMPAIGN

Britain received a lesson, without precedent, in the virtues of saving and the value of things once casually thrown away. Paper became of prime importance because it could be converted into munitions of war and the whole nation set to work to collect it. Here, beneath the flags of the United Nations, Mr. A. V. Alexander, First Lord of the Admiralty, is seen opening an exhibition designed to show the uses of waste paper as a weapon of war.

THE MIRACLE OF THE PENNY

One of the outstanding achievements in war-time money-raising has been the Red Cross Penny-a-Week Fund under the Chairmanship of Lord Southwood. The Fund, which is part of the Red Cross and St. John War Organization, was inaugurated in November, 1939. Its purpose was to enable everyone to join in the task of helping the Red Cross, in all its tremendous wartime activities. It was a simple but a great idea that appealed to the imagination of the whole nation. The results were little short of miraculous. Of the amount raised for the Red Cross from all sources, the Penny-a-Week Fund contributed about one-third of the total income. Up to the end of 1942 the contributions through the Red Cross Penny-a-Week Fund amounted to more than £4,000,000 — a truly remarkable figure when it is considered that it was all raised in pennies. The number of subscribers was over eleven millions and the weekly income more than £50,000 every week

Lord Southwood, Chairman of the Red Cross Penny-a-Week Fund.

THE NATION'S PENNIES HELPED TO SUPPLY THESE PARCELS FOR PRISONERS OF WAR
In three years of war more than 6,000,000 Red Cross Parcels were sent to British prisoners of war.

"BETTER WITHOUT THEM, I THINK"

Officers of the Ministry of Works and Planning discuss the iron railings in Parliament Square and decide they can be removed without detriment. The appearance of many streets and squares was improved by the removal of railings for scrap metal—one of the salvage economies of war and of vital use in the manufacture of steel.

EXPORT TRADE GOES ON
Crates ready for embarkation are stamped with the slogan "Britain delivers the goods."

CUTTING THE CLOTH ACCORDING TO THE COUPONS

A scheme of clothes rationing, with the object of conserving supplies and restricting expenditure to essentials, was announced by the President of the Board of Trade, Capt. Oliver Lyttelton, on June 1st, 1940. 66 coupons were allotted for 12 months, a woman's dress taking 11 points, a man's coat and trousers 21. A few modifications were made as time went on though no substantial alteration. Patches were considered patriotic, and old clothes fashionable, though women still contrived to look well-dressed. "Utility" fashions were sponsored by the Government early in 1942. These involved some standardization of material, price and style, but were well received.

NON-STOP SHIPBUILDING

The needs of wartime brook no delay. Ships and still more ships are required. There is no time for ceremony—no interval between the launching of one ship and the start of work on the next. Here, a tanker has just run down the slips. At once the keel plate of the next vessel for the stocks is slung into position and the men begin again.

War Industry

THE war was a supreme test of energy and inventiveness; in the production of armament and weapons, in the re-direction of industrial resources to new ends, and the effective use of industrial man-power.

The immense amount and variety of the material used by the fighting forces imposed on Britain's productive capacity a strain that could be met only if factories and machines hitherto employed in satisfying civilian needs, were swiftly and economically turned to the manufacture of armaments.

Great quantities of mass-production machinery, designed to perform only a few highly specialized operations, must somehow be modified so as to produce the ships, guns, tanks, planes, shells, bombs and precision instruments with which the nation must fight its battles.

Moreover, the fittest men must be withdrawn for military service from even the most essential industries; whilst from those less obviously or immediately necessary vast numbers must be taken. Somehow, then, others must be found and trained to do the work which all these lay down.

A scheme of national registration was planned to use man-power more systematically than in the last war, and to place each individual where he could be of most service. The gradual withdrawal of workers from non-essential industries followed; and, as new war-production factories were built and old ones extended, thousands of people had to be moved to the places where work was being done. There they were housed and trained for their new occupations. Simultaneously with this great switch-over, a national census of machinery was made by the Ministry of Supply, and work was allotted in accordance with the mechanical facilities of the various manufacturing organizations concerned. Finally, great numbers of men and women, hitherto quite unaccustomed to manual work, were trained in many branches of skilled industry.

It was an unprecedented re-shuffle of both human and material resources. Inevitably, there were delays, blunders, misunderstandings and inconveniences. That is not surprising. The remarkable thing is that it was done; and, on the whole, so well done that within three years of the beginning of the war the nation's output was nearing its maximum.

The Minister of Labour, Mr. Bevin, talks to munition workers.

LEARNING. Trainees at a munition works are introduced to the job by an instructor.

HARD AT WORK. Girls acetylene welding in the process of making stirrup-pump handles.

SPEEDING-UP
General view of a tank factory.

CARGO BOAT UNDER CONSTRUCTION

In clean-cut outlines, a cargo boat takes shape. Simplicity of design and speedy performance were essential.

TANKS FOR RUSSIA

British production became powerful enough to meet home needs and also to provide Britain's allies with tanks. In wartime as in peace Britain was the workshop of the world. The pledge given to Russia to send all possible support was honoured to the fullest extent although at the same time British forces had to be supplied on several battle fronts. In August, 1942, the Minister of Production could point in a broadcast on the North American Service to the fact that the Lease-Lend agreement also was not entirely one-way traffic. Britain had sent under what was known as Reciprocal Aid, things needed by America. "Reciprocal aid" said Mr. Lyttelton, "is the outcome of reciprocal aims." The United Nations shared the supplies available among themselves.

SCRAP IRON FOR WAR'S FURNACE

The wayside dumps of town and village, the railings of parks and squares, fed the mighty crucibles of Britain's steelworks with scrap metal—to be turned into the steel which pours from the ninety-ton ladle which is seen here.

They shape a white hot billet of metal for the anti-aircraft guns.

The pace quickens—in the forges of Britain's industrial centres men toil day and night.

Making Gun Barrels for Tanks.

Assembling Bren Guns.

On the outbreak of war the pace of industry quickened, but for a considerable time it did not get really going. Preparations in the early days were on a limited scale. There were also a number of problems for which no prompt solution was provided. Many months of war had gone by before British industry exerted its real power. Then, after Dunkirk the question loomed up in an urgent fashion. The equipment of nine divisions had to be suddenly replaced. A new expansion of effort was vitally necessary to match the expansion of the war. Reliance was placed on the enthusiasm of the people and well did they respond. The aim was not merely to replace lost equipment,

Inspecting a 16-in. Naval Gun.

Knocking the final blocks away before a new ship is launched.

WORKERS GOT A MOVE ON

but to attain such a mighty increase of output as had never been contemplated before. The effort was stimulated by Labour Supply Committees and Inspectors of Labour Supply. A matter that had baffled everybody for generations—how to get the skilled worker in the right place away from repetition work to where he is wanted—was substantially solved. At the same time the recruitment of a labour force from non-essential occupations was organized and numbers of people transferred from office to production work. The workshops themselves and Government training centres and technical colleges were able to turn out semi-skilled workers in four months.

Head and shoulders of the new born bomber are coaxed into position.

Huge trailers bring the centre sections to the Assembly station—a lofty echoing world of its own.

BIRTH OF A BOMBER

The engine goes home on the bulkhead of a Halifax (powered by four twelve-hundred horse power Rolls Royce engines). Other stages in the production of these giants are to be seen in the photographs on the opposite page.

STIRLINGS IN THE ASSEMBLY STATION
Like streamlined trains at some great terminus
the bomber bodies are lined up in the huge hall.

GUNS FOR OUR SHIPS

These mighty tubes which lie in long perspective are heavy naval guns in the making at a Royal Ordnance factory—soon to roar Britain's defiance at her enemies over blue water—to help maintain mastery of the seas.

WOMEN AT THE WORK BENCH

While the problems of industry were not quite the same as during the war of 1914-18—quick and easy mass production was not so general because mechanization in military operations brought with it greater complexities and consequently a greater demand for skill—the women of Britain took up unaccustomed tasks with a will to learn. Relatively, the number employed in war industry was not so great, though the total effort of women was much larger, but they quickly showed their aptitude for dealing with responsible and intricate jobs. Mannequins, dancing teachers, laboratory workers trained side by side and proved their efficiency as engineers. The deft fingers of this girl at the work bench control one of the numerous operations that go to the production of shells.

AMMUNITION PILES UP

Shells, bombs, torpedoes, endless glittering missiles come from the ordnance factories. At left, the most expensive and deadly of naval projectiles is in the making. A torpedo costs £2,000, has some 6,000 separate parts, a charge of 500 lb. of high explosive. Shells also, despite the simplicity of their appearance, have a varying internal structure. Bombs range from the small incendiary to enormous high-explosive engines of destruction. Cartridges which will be fired from a machine gun at the rate of 1,200 rounds a minute must be provided in vast numbers. To think of these things is to realize the complexity of war industry, the countless different details that must constantly be dealt with, the countless processes that are put into action.

The factory has done its part—the bombs go into the under-ground vaults of the R.A.F. ready for use.

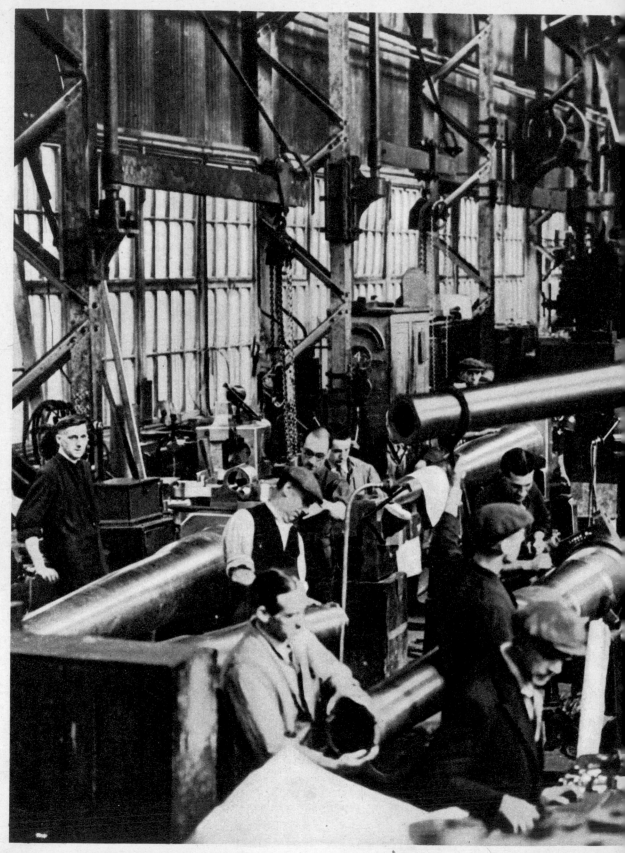

A FINISHED GUN BARREL SWINGS ACROSS AN

ORDNANCE FACTORY WORKING AT FULL PRESSURE.

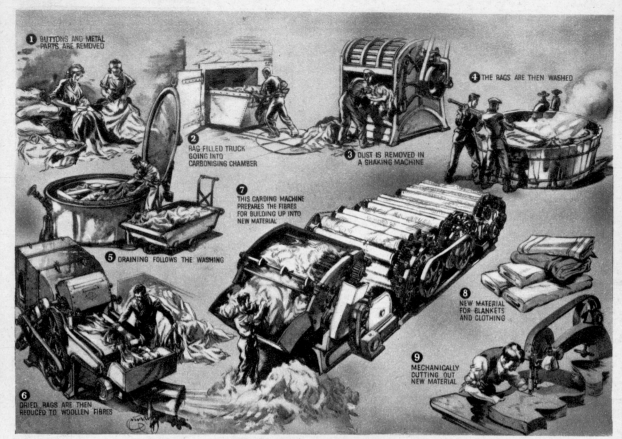

Salvage created its own industries. The separated fibres of woollen rags were made into new material as shown.

Bones passed through these processes to make many vital products from glycerine for explosives to fertilizers.

OLD INDUSTRIES AND NEW EXPANDED IN WARTIME

The war gave a new impetus to old and decayed industries, a new aspect to others. Rags, bones, waste paper and waste rubber and scrap metal became valuable raw material, the reconditioning and conversion of which to wartime use was an important industry. With the restriction of imported supply, tin was once more mined at home, and the photograph above shows miners working a compressed air drill in a reopened Cornish tin mine.

WOMEN PHOTOGRAPHERS IN THE SERVICES

Members of the W.R.N.S. (Women's Royal Naval Service) are here seen taking the air camera out of a plane after a flight. This photographic work released men for fighting jobs. Their training included a flying course.

Members of the Women's Land Army working a tractor.

Women's Work in War

WOMEN have always played their part in war; but hitherto, among civilized peoples at any rate, their work has been limited to ministries of succour and healing. Every effort has been made to protect them from danger and from active participation in offensive operations.

In our time, war had become total: total both in the sense that it was a life and death struggle for existence, and in the sense that it intimately affected every member of the community. It brought its own peculiar perils to the civilian population. It made such stringent demands on the nation's man-power that the women had to share its burdens, both of responsibility and danger, to an extent hitherto unknown.

And how magnificently they responded ! In industry they tackled successfully work that previously everyone had supposed to require both the strength and the skill of men. As uniformed auxiliaries to all branches of the fighting services, they went on active service at home and abroad. They proved that there are few war-like tasks that women could not undertake courageously and efficiently. They stood side by side with their male comrades under enemy fire, sharing with them equally the hardships, hazards and restrictions of military service and discipline.

Women trundled porters' barrows about the platforms of railway stations, drove heavy transport lorries, operated huge mechanical cranes, manned the range-finders, predictors and radio-location instruments that directed the fire of anti-aircraft batteries.

Like men, they were called up for national service, age group by age group. Those drafted to military, naval and air force auxiliary units were drilled, trained and disciplined as carefully as their male comrades. They learned how to march in companies, how to give unquestioning obedience to orders, how to cultivate the spirit of group loyalty, how to work together as teams. It was a more difficult re-adjustment for them than for men, but they accomplished it magnificently. In hospitals and dressing stations, in air-raid shelters and first-aid posts, others went their quiet way, giving comfort and care to the victims of war's savagery.

The story of women's work in war is a splendid one. Never was it more splendid than in the war that made them the working partners of men in every sort of peril and responsibility.

MANNING THE DEFENCES
Women at the range-finder on an anti-aircraft post.

GIRL FERRY PILOTS FOR THE R.A.F.

Women took on the job of ferrying new aircraft of the Royal Air Force and formed a section of the Air Transport Auxiliary Service. In this photograph women pilots are going out to take over delivery of planes at an aerodrome.

Members of the A.T.S. learn to cook in an emergency field kitchen.

A.T.S. lorry drivers service and maintain their vehicles and cover long distances under all conditions.

WOMEN'S AUXILIARY TERRITORIAL SERVICE

The A.T.S., Women's Auxiliary Territorial Service, had varied duties, its members being employed as clerks, typists, cooks, signallers, drivers, and in the hundred and one types of work required by the Army. The girls seen above who volunteered for the anti-aircraft branch of the service are receiving instruction at a gun site.

WOMEN'S AUXILIARY AIR FORCE

The W.A.A.F.s, Women's Auxiliary Air Force, played their part in many departments of the great organization which kept British planes in the air. At right, recruits at a West Country station are being fitted out with their uniforms. Below, two members of the service are on the job. They are busy refuelling aircraft. Many of the trades which are usually undertaken only by men, were ably carried out by women, who showed themselves apt as armourers, instrument repairers, flight mechanics, parachute packers, in addition to carrying out much purely administrative work.

WOMEN TECHNICIANS IN THE AIR FORCE

Air Force girls mount guns on a Spitfire. It was the principle of the R.A.F. that no job should be done by a man, if a woman could do it equally well, and the number of duties entrusted to them was thus steadily increased.

A "WREN" ON THE RIFLE RANGE

At a shore establishment of the Royal Navy, a Warrant Officer teaches the "Wrens" how to shoot.

WOMEN'S ROYAL NAVAL SERVICE

Tradition is the essence of the Royal Navy and the Women's Royal Naval Service formed in 1939, had the same name as the organization of 1917-19. As with the other auxiliaries the duties of the "Wrens" were numerous. They were clerks, teleprinters, coders, cooks, supply assistants, cinema operators and wireless mechanics. The cipher staff of each of the home commanders-in-chief was composed of W.R.N.S. officers whose work was very responsible, and the members of the service were regarded as an integral part of a ship's company. At right is a scene from "W.R.N.S." (a Ministry of Information film) showing a "Wren" at a teleprinter.

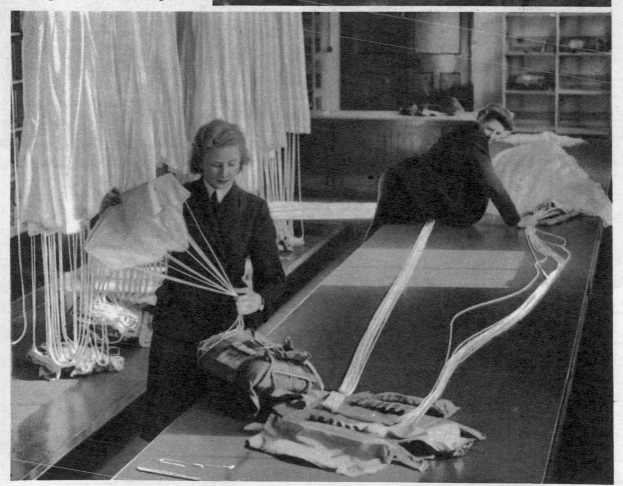

HANDY WOMEN OF THE ROYAL NAVY

"Wrens," at a Fleet Air Arm station pack parachutes in the airing room.

HANDLING A BARRAGE BALLOON

Members of the Women's Auxiliary Air Force haul on the mooring cable.

WOMEN IN CIVIL DEFENCE

In Civil Defence as with the fighting forces women took their places alongside men. They played a brave part in the work of the fire services and became keen and efficient A.R.P. wardens. Above, Mr. C. R. Attlee, M.P., talks to members of the Auxiliary Fire Service, and, below, women wardens completely equipped are going on duty.

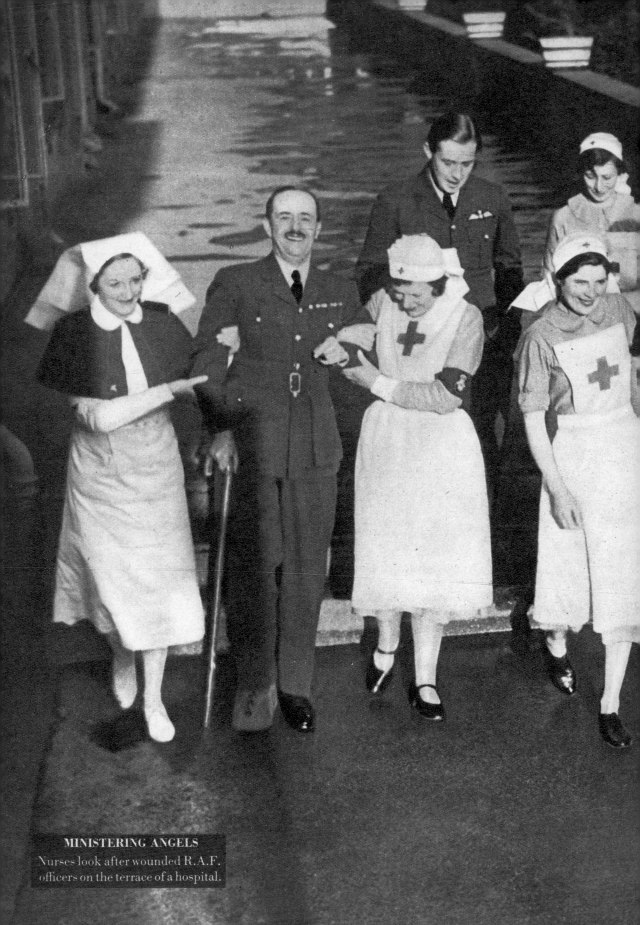

MINISTERING ANGELS
Nurses look after wounded R.A.F.
officers on the terrace of a hospital.

STREET SCENE IN COSMOPOLITAN LONDON

Norwegian patriot from the Lofoten Islands asks his way from the bus conductress.

BOY AND GIRL—A STUDY IN EXPRESSION

The District Messenger force is supplemented in wartime by young women in the uniform seen above.

WOMEN'S VARIED JOBS

Here is a selection of the many civilian wartime jobs of women. Some are employed on wastepaper collection and we see them tipping paper into the refuse cart. In the railway goods yard the woman wheels her barrow load. In the garage a girl wearing heavy Wellingtons is washing down a bus. At a railway depot they are cleaning the wheels of an engine, while another railway worker handles a heavy horse dray. It seems as if the slogan of the poster behind is not needed. The women of Britain handled their new jobs with vigour.

Three words to the WHOLE NATION
GO TO IT!

Feeding a calf.

Working a silo.

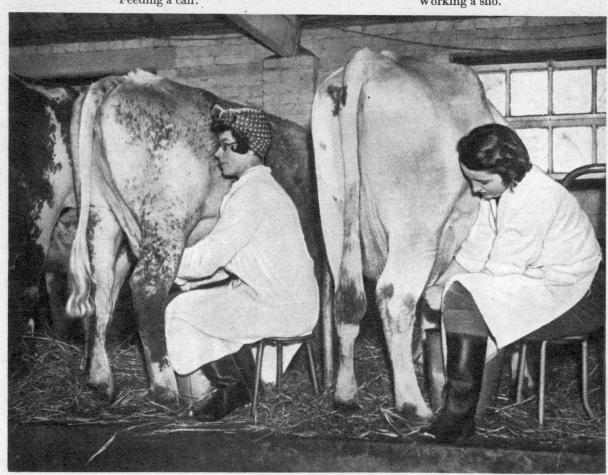

WOMEN ON THE LAND

Milking time on a dairy farm in Kent, where nearly all the work was carried out by Land Girls.

Amazons of the A.T.S. handle a two-handed saw.

WOMEN IN FACTORY AND SHIPYARD
One of the first women to work in a shipyard is here seen at a hydraulic riveting machine.

Once employed on making women's wear, these factory workers turn out barrage balloons.

Girls add finishing touches to a plane in an aircraft factory.

Members of the W.V.S. on billeting work try to find a happy home for an evacuee.

One of the many extra jobs done by W.V.S. is addressing ration books for the local authorities.

WOMEN'S VOLUNTARY SERVICE

W.V.S. centres worked for almost every local authority in the country, co-ordinating the work of women volunteers wherever they were needed. It reached a total membership of 1,000,000 by the beginning of 1942. The work done was of many kinds, including miscellaneous duties which, valuable in themselves, were not covered by any separate organization. Above, for example, is a W.V.S. canteen dispensing refreshments to harvesters. W.V.S. made effective the will to serve of women tied to their homes or able to give only their leisure.

SCHOOLBOYS IN UNIFORM.   Members of the O.T.C. give a smart salute to an officer.

Army Cadets study the map.

Britain's Youth in War

THE hope of a nation's future lies in its youth; and war lays on the community a great responsibility towards its children. That they should live in healthy surroundings, as little affected, mentally or physically, as possible, by the horrors of war, was the motive of the evacuation scheme, put into operation shortly after the war began. This in itself was a great social experiment. The town child was introduced to country life.

The young who were too old for evacuation, yet not old enough to take an adult share in the nation's war effort, were also taken care of. It was seen that their education and development must be a matter of deliberate organization. Training corps were founded for both girls and boys. Their purpose was to guide the youngsters in the principles of citizenship, inculcate a sense of social responsibility, and train them mentally and physically.

The young played their own useful part in the war effort. They helped to run local salvage and savings campaigns; some of them worked on the land during holidays from work or school; they learned to operate machines. In a hundred ways their corporate energies were directed and used.

Babies received special care. When the mothers were needed to participate in war activities of one kind or another, many crèches and day nurseries were established where the small children could be cared for while their parents were at work. Special rations were provided for them too. Oranges were reserved "For children under six only." Schools provided meals and milk. Altogether, the nation did its best for its children, during the war.

Naval officers-to-be—midshipmen's guard on the march at the Royal Naval Engineering College.

Future crews of the British Fleet—a batch of naval cadets.

WHEEL AND COMPASS INSTRUCTION
Boys of the National Sea Training Home at Wallasey are trained for life at sea.

Boys at a Nautical College study a model display of Britain's ships.

R.A.F. apprentices learn how aerial bombs are constructed at a technical training school.

Pupils of the Air Training Corps (here making model planes) receive a sound technical grounding.

FOUR BOYS WITH BUT ONE THOUGHT

Many thousands of lads, like those round this engine, trained in the A.T.C. to become the airmen of the future.

GIRLS' TRAINING CORPS AT DRILL

These girls between the ages of 14 and 17 are receiving preparatory training before joining the W.A.A.F.s.

"I can make my own bed."

Six small children take a bath. A scene at a large concentration of evacuated children in the country.

CARE OF THE EVACUATED CHILD

An open-air lesson with some interesting-looking toys absorbs these small evacuated children. Like many others, they were housed in centres, equipped in modern and scientific fashion. Education was not neglected.

TOWN CHILDREN IN THE COUNTRY

In a beautiful fifteenth-century house in Kent these children, all under five, evacuated from bombed districts of London, play happily in surroundings which have the peace and mellowed beauty of an age-old tradition.

THEY TOOK TO FARM LIFE

The young people enjoy their experience of the farm. Above are schoolgirls looking after the heifers on the school farm which they ran to help the Grow More Food Campaign. Below, a town boy and girl see to the pigs.

BRITAIN'S YOUTH ON PARADE

" Each one of you is working and preparing not only to take part in the protection of our country and of those ideals which make life worth looking forward to, but also in the disciplined efforts of the future. For then you will have to play your part as men and women in directing the contribution that we, as a nation, can and must make to the new world which will be built up after the war. . . ."

(Extract from a speech made by Sir Stafford Cripps in Nottingham at the Youth Rally, August 30, 1942.)

PRINTED IN GREAT BRITAIN BY THE SUN ENGRAVING COMPANY LIMITED, LONDON AND WATFORD.   S.343.